KENDO
—APPROACHES FOR ALL LEVELS—

Sotaro Honda
Kendo Renshi 7th-dan

Bunkasha International Corporation

FOREWORD

This book, *Kendo – Approaches For All Levels* explains the purpose and method of different types of kendo practice, as well how those different parts of training are related to each other. It also describes the correct attitude that practitioners should take in their training, and is appropriate for those at the beginning stages of practice and also practitioners who are taking up teaching roles.

Kendo is a traditional martial art in which practitioners can learn together, and from each other regardless of skill level or age, and is something that can be continued to be practised throughout one's life.

Kendo is also a physical activity in which practitioners attempt to strike parts of the body protected by armour with *shinai*. Therefore, practitioners have a responsibility to learn proper technique and avoid rough and violent striking with an attitude of respect for others.

If practitioners do kendo incorrectly, it will make others feel bad about their *keiko*, and even make them stop practising. The following is a list of points that practitioners should be careful of:

1. Practitioners must spend enough time acquiring basic techniques, especially *shinai* handling (基本重視, *kihon-jūshi*)
2. They must cultivate an attitude of mutual respect through attacking and defending (交剣知愛, *kō-ken-chi-ai*)
3. As practitioners (*shugyō-sha*), teacher and student must maintain an attitude of training together for a common purpose (師弟同行, *shi-tei-dō-gyō*)

It is often the case that the circumstances of *keiko* in other countries are different from those in Japan. People of differing ages and levels practise together in the same place at the same time. In such situations, those who are engaged in teaching are required to have sufficient knowledge of appropriate teaching methods.

I am sure that this book will make a great contribution to those practising kendo at different levels; for those at the beginning stages to develop their technical understanding, those of an intermediate level to develop interpersonal skills, and finally for those of an advanced level to develop their teaching skills.

The author, Dr. Honda was engaged in research into physical education studies at Fukuoka University of Education between 1995 and 1997. He also coached the university kendo club, and with his superb coaching skills, led the women's team to victory at the All Japan Women's

University Kendo Championships in 1996. Dr. Honda continued his studies at the University of Gloucestershire in the U.K. between 1999 and 2003, completing his Ph.D. While he was in the U.K., he was engaged in teaching at many clubs, and also made a significant contribution to the development of the British national team.

I believe that this book was written with a great amount of experience and a deep academic insight which will help many kendo practitioners around the world to develop their understanding of kendo. As such, I strongly recommend this book to all who are serious about their study of kendo.

Masatake Sumi
Kendo Hanshi 8th Dan

CONTENTS

INTRODUCTION

There are various books on kendo written or translated into English for non-Japanese practitioners. Some examples are *This is Kendo: The Art of Japanese Fencing* written by Junzo Sasamori and Gordon Warner, first published in 1964; *Fundamental Kendo* published by the All Japan Kendo Federation in 1973; *The Shambhala Guide to Kendo* written by Kiyota Minoru in 1995; *Kendo: The Definitive Guide* originally written in Japanese by Ozawa Hiroshi in 1991 and translated into English by Angela Turzynski for publication in 1997. These books introduce the historical development of kendo, philosophy, basic movements and techniques, etiquette, and Nippon Kendo Kata. The AJKF also published *Kendo Fundamentals Vols. 1 & 2* in 1994 and 1995; *Japanese-English Kendo Dictionary* in 2000 (revised in 2011); *Nippon Kendo Kata Instruction Manual* in 2002; and *The Official Guide for Kendo Instruction* in 2011. Deserving special mention is *Kendo Kata: Essence and Application* written by Inoue Yoshihiko, Hanshi 8-dan and translated by Dr. Alex Bennett (2003). This book describes the meaning of, and attitudes in *kata-geiko* in more detail than any other previous publication, helping the Western kendo practitioner understand the philosophical and technical aspects of *kata*. Moreover, it has to be mentioned that articles of various kendo related articles (original and translated) found within the pages of the *Kendo World* journal are worth reading for all Western kendo practitioners.

Nowadays, an increasing number of books are being translated from Japanese into other languages, and some publications are actually penned by non-Japanese authors in addition to the books mentioned above. For example, *Looking at a Far Mountain: A Study of Kendo Kata* written by Paul Budden in 1992; *Herding the Ox: The Martial Arts as Moral Metaphor*; and *Complete Kendo* written by Dr. John. J. Donohue in 1998 and 1999; *The Heart of Kendo* written by Darrell Max Craig in 1999.

After reading these books I was amazed at the extent of kendo's internationalisation. All such publications are invaluable sources of information to help Western kendo practitioners improve their skills, and develop a keen understanding of the spiritual and philosophical aspects of kendo.

To contribute to this trend, I was also thinking of translating my teacher's (Hanshi 8-dan Masatake Sumi's) book called *Nendai-betsu Keiko-hō Michi no Kaori* (Kendo for Every Age: The Scent of the Way). It introduces ways of practising with each different age group, and I had hoped that by completing the translation it would contribute to helping Western kendo practitioners in the future. However, upon talking to one of my kendo friends, Mr. George McCall (former British national team member who now resides in Japan), he told me "Sotaro, we don't normally start doing kendo when we are young like Japanese. Also, the frequency of *keiko* and opportunities to practise with highly graded *sensei*, and many other circumstances are very different between Japan and the U.K. So, it would not be so useful to translate a book written primarily for Japanese kendo practitioners." I felt as if something had hit me when I heard this from George. I re-examined books translated and published about kendo so far, and then reconsidered how kendo has been practised in Western countries until now.

Undoubtedly, these books provide Western kendo practitioners with great knowledge of what kendo is, how it is practised, and what philosophies lay behind this form of athletic culture. However, it would be helpful if there was more access to ideas for practising and teaching kendo that takes into consideration the age they start kendo, frequency of *keiko*, and various other cultural or social circumstances surrounding kendo in Western countries.

In the summer of 2003, it was quite a coincidence that I was given an opportunity by George to be introduced to Dr. Alex Bennett, of whose work I had been admiring for a long time. He kindly offered me an opportunity to write a series of articles for *Kendo World*. I was honoured to receive this opportunity, and wrote articles related to *keiko* methodology for Western kendo practitioners, making use of my experience of practising and teaching kendo in both Japan and the U.K. It is those articles, and some others that I wrote for the British Kendo Association, that this book is comprised.

CHAPTER 1

A COMPARISON OF CIRCUMSTANCE

1. Introduction

In this first chapter, I will describe how kendo is practised in Japan based on my experience and observations, and will use this as a basis to take up some points that need to be considered when practising and teaching kendo in Western countries.

2. How Kendo is Practised in Japan

Many Japanese people start practising kendo when they are primary school students (6 through to 12 years of age), or junior high school students (12-15 years of age). At primary school, most kendo students practise between one and half hours to two hours each session at their own local *dōjō*, two or three times a week on average. Primary school students spend a lot of time training in the fundamental techniques, or *kihon-geiko*.

At junior high school, students usually practise at their school kendo club in addition to a local *dōjō*. However, students who start kendo for the first time at junior high school mostly just train at the school kendo club. In the Japanese school system, junior high schools are often affiliated with a senior high school giving junior and senior high school pupils opportunities to train together. The training regime by this stage becomes increasingly intensive with many clubs practising more than five times a week. Top level students will have already attained quite a high level of technical skill and tactical ability. Moreover, in spite of their young age, some students decide to concentrate solely on kendo as a career path, rather than as something to 'enjoy', and thus tend to neglect other activities such as study.

At senior high school (15-18 years of age), most students only practise at their high school clubs. Without a doubt, high school clubs are where the hardest and most gruelling training sessions are conducted. Most clubs practise more than five or six times a week and participate in a harsh training regime that is little short of death defying. As well as repeated *kihon-geiko*, they practise *kakari-geiko* over and over as it is commonly accepted that this is the most effective method for improvement. At strong high school clubs, students are required to make a very serious commitment to club kendo life. In fact, this not only applies to students, but also to parents who are expected to provide moral and logistical support as much as possible. The amount of training conducted by students of the same age group who do not belong to school clubs but practise only at a local *dōjō* pales in comparison as far as intensity is concerned, and is generally considered to be no more than a hobby.

There has been much criticism directed at high school kendo teaching methodologies and also the overtly competitive fighting style. To give some examples, high school kendo instructors have been subjected to strong criticisms for their tendency to force their students to practise too much without giving them enough rest or a chance to re-hydrate, and focusing on winning at all costs. Similarly, students are criticised for their messy style of engagement that ignores taking the centreline (*chūshin*) and focuses on hitting opponents relying only on speed and using unorthodox or underhanded techniques to score points.

When high school students progress to university, they are required to make a qualitative conversion from so-called "high school kendo" to "university kendo". In other words, they are expected to evolve from "speed kendo" to a style based on attempting to strike through dominating the *chūshin*. Also, the span of responsibility changes drastically, and parents play little or no role whatsoever other than sending money for rent and food!

At university level, planning and organising training and tournaments are left entirely up to the students. Duration and frequency of *keiko* differs between universities. Some university clubs have over one-hundred members and train almost every day. Some universities train twice a day with *asa-geiko* (early morning practice) and *keiko* in the evening as well. Often the instructor's attention will be directed at students who entered the university on a sports scholarship based their outstanding *shiai* (competition) results at high school. Ordinary students are normally not given any chance to take part in major tournaments while at university.

On the other hand, there are some universities who do not have gifted kendo scholarship students among their ranks, but through hard *keiko* are able to improve their kendo significantly, and on occasion beat strong universities even though they are underdogs. It is always exciting to see this when it happens. Yet again, some universities place emphasis on "enjoying" kendo as a social activity, and do not take tournaments so seriously (at least not as seriously as some of the drinking parties!)

After graduating, involvement with kendo depends entirely on the company the graduate enters. Some people are able to practise as a part of their job, like the police for example. Some people can train at work as members of their company kendo club. Then again, many people find little time for *keiko* because of their busy work schedules. The reality is that after graduation, the majority of *kendō-ka* find little time for anything more than an odd hour of *ji-geiko* here and there, if they're lucky. In order to continue kendo, these people require a positive attitude to look for a place, time, and people with whom they can practise, no matter how sporadic their opportunities may be.

Some people who are very keen attend *asa-geiko* sessions before going to work, and will go anywhere they can participate in *keiko* with high grade instructors. There are also many people who did not like kendo when they were training as students due to the high pressure to succeed, but gradually come to enjoy kendo after graduating. At university, the student is often 'forced' into hard kendo and put under strong pressure to perform in tournaments. After exiting such an environment, they are now able to control their own pace of training without feeling any pressure or group obligation.

Here, I should also mention people who teach children in their spare time at community *dōjō* after work. Such people devote their spare time to teaching children, and spend many weekends taking them to regional tournaments. It is no exaggeration to say that much of the development of Japanese kendo is based on the efforts and dedication of volunteers.

3. Practising and Teaching Kendo in Western Countries

Compared to Japanese, the majority of Westerners commence their study of kendo much later in life. For example, in the case of the Great Britain, the average age for passing *shodan* is 31 years (European Kendo Federation, 2001). From this, it is possible to surmise that the average age British people start kendo is in their late twenties. The frequency of *keiko* is likely to be once or twice a week for most people, and three or four times a week for extra keen practitioners. People of various ages, ranks, and experience often practise together in Western countries, and it is difficult for teachers to organise training sessions so that all participants receive sufficient or adequate training to satisfy individual needs.

It is also difficult for teachers, especially higher grades, to engage in *keiko* with people of the same level or higher. Moreover, it is not easy for beginners in the upper age bracket to improve whilst training together with beginners who are much younger. (This also applies to Japanese people who start kendo in their senior years).

As for the training environment in the *dōjō*, the floor is normally harder than in Japan, and it is hard to find a place suitable for the basic stamping footwork (*fumikomi-ashi*). As for the *Nippon Kendo Kata*, Western practitioners seem to spend more time studying this aspect of kendo when they are beginners than Japanese. It is sometimes mentioned in Japanese kendo magazines that Japanese people who have visited the West are impressed by the level of *kata* proficiency, and feel acutely embarrassed with their comparatively poor skills.

I am in no way implying that overall *keiko* in Western countries is insufficient and needs to be done the "Japanese way". It is never too late to start kendo, and practising almost every day is not necessarily good. In Japan, the problem of young people chained to club activities (*keiko, shiai-geiko, taikai*) has been the focal point of active and heated discussions for quite some time. What I would like to stress here is that it is not always effective for Western kendo practitioners to follow the Japanese process of learning kendo. It would be more suitable for Westerners to modify and devise suitable *keiko* methodology with due consideration to the age of the student and frequency of *keiko* opportunities.

4. Summary

An important point in need of consideration is to make amply clear the purpose of each *keiko* session. One *keiko* needs to be connected with the next, so that the student is able to train with a clear understanding of each session, rather than following the typical Japanese style where skills and understanding are developed gradually by experience and constant repetition. Of course, many readers already know this, and have been training and teaching to great effect in their respective *dōjō* given the comparatively limited opportunities and resources available in the West. In the ensuing chapters, however, I would like to develop ideas of how kendo can be practised in Western countries with optimum efficiency.

CHAPTER 2

FOOTWORK

1. Introduction

In the previous chapter I introduced some books about kendo that have been translated into English or written by non-Japanese authors. I also considered what is important when contributing materials for Western kendo practitioners. Moreover, I mentioned that I was interested in developing methods of practising and teaching kendo for non-Japanese practitioners, taking into consideration the age they start kendo, the frequency of their *keiko* and other circumstances and customs that are different from Japan. In this chapter, I will introduce my ideas for *ashi-sabaki* (footwork) and cutting. These are the first things that beginners learn, and are also essential elements even for experienced people to continue practising.

2. Ashi-Sabaki

There are four types of basic *ashi-sabaki* in kendo. They are called *ayumi-ashi, okuri-ashi, hiraki-ashi* and *tsugi-ashi* (see figure 1). First and foremost, it is important that the instructor provides a clear picture of how mastering footwork is inextricably linked with more advanced aspects of training such as *waza-geiko* (technique practice), *ji-geiko* (sparring) and *shiai* (matches). Instructors must clearly demonstrate the various movements, and make their students understand the relationship between each kind of footwork and the circumstances in which each is employed.

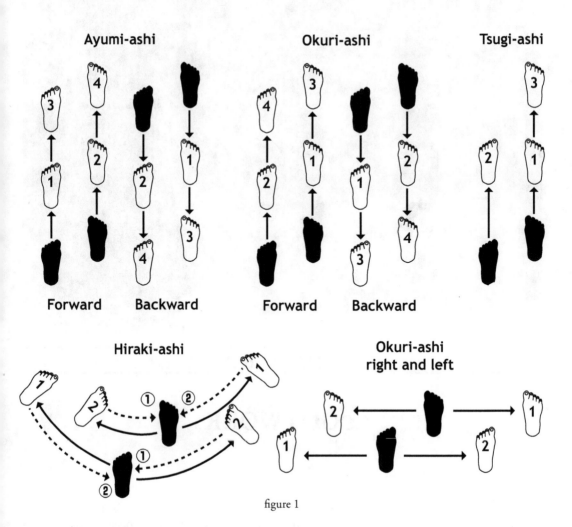

figure 1

3. The Problem

After realising the fundamental importance of footwork, the next steps are to understand which foot should be used as a source of power, and to recognise the specific function of each foot. This is especially relevant when practising *okuri-ashi* which is closely related to *fumikiri* and *fumikomi*, and will be introduced in a later chapter.

People tend to follow two set patterns when practising *okuri-ashi*. The first is "*ichi*" (move the right foot forward), "*ni*" (pull up the left foot), "*san*" (move the left foot back), "*shi*" (pull back the right foot). The second is "*ichi*" (move the right foot forward and pull up the left foot), "*ni*" (move the left foot back and pull back the right foot). As a result of practising these two patterns, a common problem is that the left foot has a tendency to lag behind. This problem becomes more obvious when continuous steps are linked together, for example when doing *okuri-ashi* from one side of the *dōjō* to the other. Needless to say, the problem is accentuated with the introduction of *fumikomi*. In this case, the left side of the body gets left behind, and the practitioner ends up going forwards but the direction the body is facing becomes diagonal.

The combination of the lagging left foot and diagonal posture results in a jerky movement. This unfortunate problem is a result of practitioners simply looking at and copying the movement of others. It is difficult to understand how someone is achieving the smooth sliding movement just by watching. If the practitioner clearly understands which foot is being used to push off with, and where the power is coming from, they will be able to do *okuri-ashi* properly. The following presents one way of solving this problem.

4. One Solution

Let us re-examine the function of the left and right feet. Thinking that *okuri-ashi* is just "moving the right foot forward and then pulling up the left foot" is not enough. When moving forward with *okuri-ashi*, practitioners should understand that the right foot moves because the left leg is doing the pushing. When pulling up the left foot, it is the right leg which is doing the pulling. Equally when the left leg pushes, the right foot moves forward. When the right leg pulls, the left foot is pulled up.

To describe this process in detail: 1) push the floor with the left leg (as a result the right foot moves forward); 2) straighten the right leg (as a result the left foot is pulled up); 3) after step two, immediately push the floor with the left leg and repeat the process again.

The movement of the left foot will improve if the practitioner understands the function of each foot in this way. First it is best to start with big and slow movements. The head will bob up and down but this is not a problem. As movement becomes smoother and smaller this will correct itself if too much focus is put on keeping the head from moving up and down at this stage, it results in jerky movement. If you have ever been ice-skating, then you will already have experienced a situation where the leading foot is pushed forwards by the power of the trailing leg. *Okuri-ashi* follows the same principle.

Details will be explained later, but keep in mind that this principle is closely related to mastering *fumikiri* and *fumikomi*. This way of thinking about footwork needs to be introduced during the beginning stages of kendo in order to serve as a foundation for further practice.

The next point to be considered is to encourage practising *ashi-sabaki* while interacting with a partner. It is more fun and realistic for students to pair off and focus on their distancing, the height of their *shinai* and *metsuke* (gaze) etc. than just having the instructor standing in front of them. For example, two people facing each other can check their *chūdan-no-kamae* (posture, stance, *shinai* height etc.). They then decide who moves first (side A) and who follows (side B). When A takes one step forward, B takes one step backward. When A takes one step to the right, B takes one step to the left. Both sides, especially side B, must try to maintain the same distance between each other (*maai*). Thus, practitioners start by moving one step forward, backward, right or left, and then gradually increase the number of steps.

It is also important for teachers to take this opportunity to make their students understand the importance of keeping 'en' in *keiko*. En is the mental connection and the relationship between yourself and your partner during *keiko*. Maintaining *en* during *keiko* is a fundamental requirement and it is the teacher's responsibility to make sure that students understand this. It is closely related to understanding and practising *kentai-itchi* which will be introduced later.

Next, learners should be encouraged to take diagonal steps as well. This is followed by the next stage in which they can move freely in any direction and can take as many steps as they like. At this point, both sides are encouraged not only to use *okuri-ashi* but also other types of footwork such as *ayumi-ashi*, *hiraki-ashi*, and *tsugi-ashi* by keeping their knees slightly bent and their posture straight so as to master smooth and effortless *ashi-sabaki*.

At the final stage of this practice, A attempts to keep control of *chūshin* (the centre) and break B's *chūshin* by using *harai*, *osae* and *maki* techniques when the *maai* gets too close. One of the important objectives of this exercise is not only to master *okuri-ashi* moving forwards, but also other *ashi-sabaki* for moving in all directions.

For the most part, in *waza-geiko* we tend to move forwards and backwards, especially forwards, using *okuri-ashi*. However, if this is the limit of one's footwork repertoire, one's ability to move in various directions during *ji-geiko* or *shiai* will be severely inhibited. Thus, the objective of practising footwork with a partner is to acquire smooth body movement utilising all types of footwork for movement in all directions, and also aims to encourage relaxed but firm *tenouchi* (grip on the *shinai*), to maintain proper posture at all times, and to control the centre.

5. Cutting

In kendo we are required to 'cut' with the *shinai*, not simply 'touch' or 'hit'. Of course, this should be taken as the ideal rather than in a literal sense. We consider our *shinai* to be a sword and try to strike with emphasis on correct *hasuji* (striking with the cutting edge of the blade) with the feeling of attempting to 'cut' our target. Having said that, I would not actually be able to provide a specific answer if asked "Then, what is a strike that 'cuts', and what is not?" In kendo, if a strike is executed with appropriate timing while taking advantage of a clear opening, we should have the feeling of having made a good cut or having been cut, even if the attack is light.

On the other hand, if the attack is made randomly when the striking opportunity was not clear, we tend not to acknowledge it as a good cut even if it is a heavy strike. As we develop our skills and understanding of kendo, we learn to share the same feeling of 'cutting' or 'being cut' with many people. It requires a lot of *keiko* experience, and takes a long time, but continuing hard training is the only way to reach this understanding. With this mind, I would like to introduce an idea that helps beginners understand and practise *suburi* and actual striking with good posture in connection with *ashi-sabaki*, and the idea of making a 'good cut'.

Imagine that there is an opponent in front of you when you do the practice swings in *suburi*, and try to 'cut' that opponent. You should transfer power from your shoulders to elbows, from elbows to wrists, and then to the *shinai*. Do not just wave the *shinai* up and down aimlessly.

Always snap your left foot up without leaving it lagging behind, remembering that source of power for this snap is the straightening of the right leg. *Hikitsuke* occurs just after the strike and stamp (*fumikomi*). Without *hikitsuke* the action of 'cutting' cannot be completed. Figure 2 shows this idea diagrammatically. *Hikitsuke* also enables readiness for the next movement.

Stage 1 shows the hit on the opponent. The action of 'cutting' is completed after the left foot is brought up, and posture is stabilised as demonstrated in Stage 2. It might be easier to understand if you imagine how a knife is used when you cut bread; you cannot cut by pushing down from the top. You have to slice it. Bringing your left foot up as in Stage 2 completes this 'cutting' action in kendo. This may not be the most appropriate way to explain cutting, but it will provide beginners with an opportunity to grasp the feeling of cutting and the relationship between *ashi-sabaki* and striking.

Stage 1. Hitting only   **Stage 2. Hitting to Cutting**

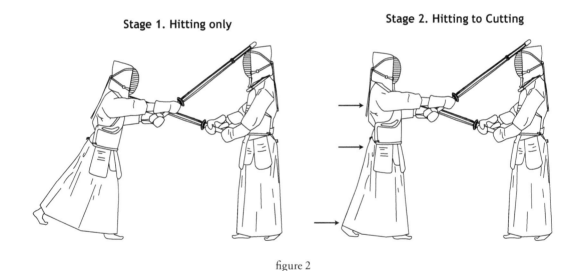

figure 2

6. Summary

In this chapter, I introduced my ideas for practising and teaching *ashi-sabaki* and the all-important cutting action. I did not describe the technical aspects of each exercise in great detail, because my intention was to show methods of practising and teaching footwork and cutting that are interconnected, and are also relevant to *keiko*. In the next chapter, I will present ways of practising and teaching *fumikomi* and *hikitsuke* for people who start kendo later in life, or who have problems with their knees. Both of these situations are often encountered in Western countries. Also, I will offer some suggestions on how kendo can be kept injury-free.

CHAPTER 3

KŪKAN-DATOTSU AND KIHON-UCHI

1. Introduction

In this chapter, I will discuss *fumikiri, fumikomi* and *kihon-uchi* (basic cutting). In addition, I will suggest how kendo practitioners can reduce the risk of injury in training.

In Chapter 2, I introduced some ideas for practising and teaching *ashi-sabaki* and cutting. Some of the main points I emphasised were to re-examine how the left and right foot should interact when practising *okuri-ashi*, and to practise not only *okuri-ashi* for moving forward and backward, but also *ayumi-ashi, hiraki-ashi, tsugi-ashi*, to encourage smooth movement in all directions. Another important point in *suburi* and striking is to create a 'cutting' action through the *hikitsuke* action of the left foot. Also, when practising and teaching basics emphasis should be placed on keeping a sense of connection *en* with your partner in your movements. This chapter will look at ways to optimise footwork in basic training.

2. Fumikiri and Fumikomi

Simply put, *fumikiri* is the push-off or the leap forward using the left foot when in *chūdan*, *migi-jōdan* or *sei-nitō*; and *fumikomi* refers to the stamp on the floor with the entire sole of the right foot. The left and right feet are opposite when in *hidari-jōdan* and *gyaku-nitō*. The *shinai* should strike at the same time as the foot stamps down. Bringing the back foot up immediately by straightening the right leg (*hikitsuke*), maintaining good posture, and demonstrating *zanshin* are also important components for correct striking. Incidentally, when a striking movement is observed closely, the *shinai* actually makes impact first, and the *fumikomi* stamp occurs a split-second afterwards. Nevertheless, for all intents and purposes, we consider that they occur simultaneously, and this is what practitioners should strive for in their own training and when teaching others.

3. The Problem

Fumikiri and *fumikomi* are unique and unusual movements which are difficult to master. Beginners often mistakenly perform the striking sequence as follows:

> *Kamae* → swinging the *shinai* back with not enough *fumikiri*, the upper-body starts leaning forward → *fumikomi* → swinging the *shinai* down → striking → moving forward with clumsy *okuri-ashi*

This jerky sequence is related to three factors. The first is a lack of understanding of the roles of the left and right feet that were mentioned in the previous chapter. Second is the failure to apply the role of each foot in *okuri-ashi* to the more dynamic movements of *fumikiri* and *fumikomi*. The final factor is a lack of coordination between the movements of the upper and lower body. Many novice practitioners will continually experience this difficulty. They keep trying to improve their coordination by practising over and over again with only gradual improvement. Some finally master the action on their own, and are able to perform it automatically without thinking. However, others may fail to show much improvement despite regular practice.

4. One Solution

To practise *fumikiri* and *fumikomi*, I suggest starting with *ayumi-ashi* (ordinary footsteps) rather than *okuri-ashi*. For example, when striking *men* from *chūdan*, take a regular step forward with your left foot first and swing your *shinai* up at the same time. When you feel your weight rest on your left foot (this should be when the *shinai* is above your head), push your body forward, swing your *shinai* down, quickly move your right leg forward and slap your foot onto the floor. The idea of practising like this is that the right knee moves directly forward, not in an upward motion. After striking, continue moving forward with *okuri-ashi*. Begin this exercise slowly with relaxed shoulders and knees. At this stage, the head may be moving up and down, but is not a great concern. It is much more important to emphasise the roles of the left and right feet. Try to lift yourself up immediately after stamping your right foot. Your left foot will be brought up naturally and you will be able to keep moving forward with smooth *okuri-ashi*.

In summary, practitioners should be aware of the following points:
- Keep your posture straight during all of the movements even if your head is moving up and down
- Stretch your arms out during the strike
- Look straight ahead, not down in front of you

- Drive off from your left foot, moving your right foot forward, and then perform the *fumikomi* and strike at the same time
- Make a smooth transition into *okuri-ashi* without stopping or slowing down after the strike

When beginners perform this exercise, they should concentrate on their movements rather than worrying about shouting. Their focus should be on improving their swinging, pushing and stamping coordination. Instructors should also stress the importance of beginners visualising their strike 'cutting' from the top of the head down to the nose. When you are comfortable with this exercise, move onto *fumikiri* and *fumikomi* practice using *okuri-ashi* in the following steps:

1. Move your right foot forward using the power of your left foot without lifting your *shinai*
2. Raise your *shinai* above your head as you bring your left foot up by straightening the right leg
3. Move forwards by pushing off with your left foot and stepping out with your right leg. Swing the *shinai* down to cut and stamp with your right foot at the same time
4. Lift yourself up by straightening the right leg, then keep moving forward
5. Turn around in an **anti-clockwise direction by pivoting on the right foot** then immediately take *kamae* ready to attack or defend

Always be aware of the points listed previously. At first, there is no need to do this exercise quickly; the important thing is to 'cut' *men* even when practising with large and slow movements.

Drilling *fumikiri* and *fumikomi* does not have to be limited to the *dōjō*; there are many opportunities for you to practise in daily life. For example, when you are walking, imagine pushing your body and floating your right foot forward. When walking up stairs, try to lift yourself up by feeling the tension in your right thigh. As I mentioned previously, *fumikiri* and *fumikomi* are unusual movements. If you do not have many opportunities to practise them in *dōjō* training, take every opportunity to rehearse *fumikiri* and *fumikomi* outside of the *dōjō*. Just make sure other people are not watching!

5. Moving to Kihon-uchi

The exercises outlined above are known as *kūkan-datotsu* – practice which refers to striking "empty air" as opposed to actually striking a training partner. After you can perform "*kamae* – steps 1) and 2) above – *men* cut and stamp – *okuri-ashi* – *kamae*" as a smooth sequence, I recommend further improving your *fumikiri* and *fumikomi* in groups by attacking targets provided by *motodachi*.

Generally, training in which striking or thrusting targets provided by a *motodachi* is called "*kihon-uchi*" (basic striking or cutting). Practitioners should realise however, that *kihon-uchi* encompasses much more than just correct *shinai* manipulation. Attacking with correct *kihon-uchi* requires (i) smooth *ashi-sabaki* before and after the attack; (ii) proper *fumikiri*; and, (iii) proper coordination of the attacking and *fumikomi* motion. *Fumikiri* and *fumikomi* are very important parts of *kihon-uchi*. Beginners should repeat *kihon-uchi* to build the foundations for their movements before they start wearing *bōgu*. More experienced practitioners should continue doing *kihon-uchi* to reflect upon their basics, and make those foundations even stronger.

6. Practice

The *kihon-uchi* exercise described below is practised in groups of 5 or 6 people taking turns with a *motodachi* wearing *dō* and *tare*. People with different levels of experience can learn through observation and mutual feedback by doing these drills in groups.

Motodachi and *kakarite* start by facing each other in *kamae* at *tōma* distance, and the *motodachi* then provides a target after establishing "*en*" with *kakarite*. To maintain *en* between *kakarite* and *motodachi*, the *motodachi* should apply pressure on *kakarite* throughout the whole exercise with the feeling, "I will attack you if you give me even the slightest opportunity!" *Motodachi*'s face, body and feet should be pointing towards *kakarite* wherever they move. Even after *kakarite* strikes, *motodachi* should turn around and apply pressure, forcing them to maintain awareness and concentration throughout the whole exercise.

To practise *men*, *motodachi* offers their *shinai* as a target by taking one step to their right side (*kakarite*'s left) and holding the *shinai* at the target height corresponding to the physical height of *kakarite*. For *kote* attacks, the *motodachi* moves to the right again and holds their *shinai* at the height of *kakarite*'s wrist. For *dō* attacks, *motodachi* raises their arms to offer a normal *dō* target. For *tsuki* attacks, *motodachi* takes one step to either side and holds the *shinai* vertically with the *tsuka* at the top and the *kensen* at the bottom. To do this, hold the *shinai* just below the *tsuba* and extend your arm so that the middle of *tsuka* comes to the throat height of each *kakarite*.

In these instances, both *men* and *kote* should follow the same 1)~5) sequence as outlined on page 15. For *dō* attacks, *kakarite* pushes his or her whole body with the left foot, but twists slightly to the right during Step 3). *Fumikomi* for *dō* attacks should not be as strong as those for *men* and *kote*. The body and the right foot should be pointing in the direction in which *kakarite* wishes to move after cutting through. These movement modifications provide sufficient space to cut accurately and follow through with ease.

There are two kinds of footwork that *kakarite* can use when cutting through. Firstly, by bringing up the left foot quickly and continuing to move through with *okuri-ashi*; or secondly, as in Kata No. 7 (*Nanahon-me*), move the left foot forward in *ayumi-ashi* and then continue with *okuri-ashi*.

For *gyaku-dō* attacks, *kakarite* approaches as before, but Step 3) is modified again. The strike is made by pushing the right side of the body forward and twisting slightly to the left. *Fumikomi* for *gyaku-dō* attacks are also not as strong as those for *men* and *kote*; but a big step is required with the right foot and the left foot is not brought up when striking. After striking, *kakarite* pushes away with the right foot to step back, takes one more step using *okuri-ashi* without stopping or slowing down (right-left-right), and then resumes *kamae* again at the *tōma* interval. The direction that *kakarite* moves after striking can be changed to go backwards, diagonally backwards to the left, or forward to the left as they further develop their basics.

For *tsuki* attacks, *kakarite* should first slide their right foot forward using the power of the left foot, bring their left foot up without moving the *shinai*, push off with the left foot, and take a big step forwards with the right. At the same time, both arms should be extended towards the target, twisting them slightly inwards to perform a two-handed *morote-zuki*. Alternatively, to perform a one-handed *katate-zuki*, only the left arm is extended and the bent right arm is pulled back to the right side to protect the *dō*.

The focus initially should be upon *kakarite* pushing off with the left foot correctly. Therefore, at first I recommend that *kakarite* leaves their left foot behind for a while. At the next level, after coordinating the push-off from the left foot with the thrusting extension of the arm(s), *kakarite* can then bring up their left foot and take *kamae* after thrusting. *Kakarite* should only worry about *tsuki* accuracy once they can perform these basic motions properly.

Group *kihon-uchi* practice like this should be performed with big, slow movements, paying particular attention to the coordination of footwork and striking. Also, whether striking or thrusting, practitioners must ensure that their left hand does not veer off the centreline of their body; it should only move up and down the centre. Another point for instructors to keep in mind is that they probably mastered basic *ashi-sabaki*, *fumikiri* and *fumikomi* a long time ago, and these movements are already automatic for them. When teaching they can probably demonstrate good examples of what beginners should be working towards, however, they may fall into the trap of not being able to explain how to perform the movements properly, and become frustrated when club members cannot do it themselves. Often instructors like this simply leave their students to their own devices hoping they will acquire the skills in time.

I suggest you remind yourself of what it is like to be a beginner by assuming a *kamae* with the opposite foot to the one you normally have forwards, reverse your grip so that it is opposite to how you normally hold the *shinai*, and then attempt to strike.

7. Physical Difficulties with Footwork

The movements of *fumikiri* and *fumikomi* themselves, and the methods of practice I described here are generally recommended for people who have no problem with their ankles and knees; these exercises can prove difficult and painful for those with bad joints. So, should these people quit kendo or not even start in the first place? Of course not! I think that one of the most significant aspects of kendo is that people can start and enjoy practice with others irrespective of differences in age, physique and gender, and they can continue to train throughout their lives. However, it is necessary for such people to learn and practise alternative *ashi-sabaki*, as well as developing effective teaching approaches.

The current approach to learning and teaching kendo is based on the premise that practitioners have no injuries, and largely use *okuri-ashi* for moving and *fumikiri* and *fumikomi* during the execution of an attack. Some people may have the perception that if *okuri-ashi* is not being used, then what is being performed is not really kendo.

I would like to briefly describe some ideas with which people experiencing problems because of age, injury or difficulty of movement can be taught and encouraged to practise kendo. Those who have physical difficulty performing *fumikiri* and *fumikomi* should use *suri-ashi*. Using *suri-ashi* movement in all directions is possible through a combination of *ayumi-ashi*, *hiraki-ashi*, *tsugi-ashi*, as well as *okuri-ashi*.

An attack with *suri-ashi* is not as fast as with *fumikiri*, and the resulting strike may not be as strong unless one has good *tenouchi*. However, big striking actions with well-controlled *suri-ashi* movements will enable one to perform various attacking combinations from different directions. An example is to swing the *shinai* up as if to strike *men* using *okuri-ashi*, but then step forward with your left foot using *ayumi-ashi* and strike *dō*. Another variation would be to slide forward with *okuri-ashi*, strike *kote*, lift the *shinai* up as if to strike *men*, but then step forward with your left foot using *ayumi-ashi* and strike *dō*. These are only two examples, and many other combinations are possible. If you can successfully feint a movement, your opponent may become confused and your next straight attack may be successful.

Instructors should take into consideration each student's age and physical condition, and try to bring out everyone's best kendo by avoiding stereotypical teaching patterns. Of course, important fundamentals such as correct posture and *hasuji* must be observed by all, and instructors should help everyone learn proper basics. However it is also the responsibility of the instructor to work as a mediator in suggesting how basics can be applied in each student's practice.

To achieve this, instructors must be creative and welcome the challenge of developing new techniques from fundamental movements. Instructors should also make their students appreciate that there are many different types of kendo, and show how to train with people who employ them. This is an excellent learning experience and increases the general awareness of the effects that age and experience have on ones kendo training.

I attended a grading up to 5-dan level at a seminar held outside London in the summer of 2004. One of the candidates who was over 60 years old passed his 3-dan examination. This particular practitioner had a bad knee and could not perform *sonkyo*, *fumikiri* and *fumikomi*; however his smooth *suri-ashi* movement and large and skilful *shinai* action overwhelmed his opponents who were almost two generations younger. His posture was straight, and he struck with correct *hasuji* making a nice sound in the *dōjō*. Watching this grading reminded me what a wonderful thing kendo is.

8. Injuries

Finally I would like to briefly turn to the topic of injuries. Many injuries that occur in kendo have been discussed in "Kendo Clinic" articles by Dr. Arima in *Kendo World*. These articles discuss what kinds of injuries occur, and how they can be treated. Naturally, the most important thing is preventing the injury from occurring in the first place. Some people seem to believe that you will not injure yourself if you perform kendo "correctly"; however kendo contains many unique and unnatural movements that must be performed repeatedly over the course of many years. This brings with it the risk of over-use or repetitive-strain injuries.

In recent years many different kinds of protectors and aids have become available such as heel pads, *tabi*, knee braces, wrist and forearm protectors and bracing tapes, but it is often the case that practitioners only start using these after they experience pain or injury. Most people feel there is no point in purchasing these aids if they have no sensation of strain or pain. I would urge people to think about the long-term picture. Those who want to continue with kendo throughout their lifetime may benefit from preventing any potential injuries occurring in the first place.

9. Summary

So far, I have introduced methods of practising and teaching basic footwork and cutting that practitioners can perform without wearing *men* in most instances. In the next chapter, I will introduce methods of training and teaching in interactive striking situations wearing full *bōgu*. The discussion will focus on the methodology and usefulness of *kirikaeshi* and *uchikomi-geiko*.

CHAPTER 4

KIRIKAESHI AND UCHIKOMI-GEIKO

1. Introduction

So far, I have introduced some training methods that students of kendo can use in their first stages of practice without wearing *men*. In Chapter 4, I would like to discuss some methods involving actual striking situations with others in full *bōgu*. I will introduce the concept of performing strikes that start out "big, slow, and accurate", develop to be "big, quick, and accurate" and finally become "small, quick, and accurate". The focus will be on the above concept as it relates to *kirikaeshi* and *uchikomi-geiko,* and its place in kendo practice.

2. Re-examining Kirikaeshi

In most of the kendo clubs that I have seen both in Japan and in Western countries, *keiko* for experienced practitioners generally starts with *mokusō*, a warm-up, *suburi* and then *kirikaeshi* after donning *men*. Some clubs may include *Nippon Kendo Kata* or "Training Method for Fundamental Kendo Techniques with a Bokuto" at the start of training. Beginners, it seems, are allowed to start practising *kirikaeshi* with experienced *motodachi* when they are able to co-ordinate the movements of their upper and lower body through practising *ashi-sabaki*, *suburi* and *kūkan-datotsu*. What this means is that, in most cases, *kirikaeshi* is the first actual striking exercise involving others in full *bōgu*.

If a club member is late for *keiko* it is reasonable to assume that they will do *kirikaeshi* before joining general *keiko*. *Kirikaeshi* is also significant in many clubs in that it marks the end of *keiko* just before taking off *men* as well as the start of *keiko*. It is said that "kendo starts with *rei* and ends with *rei*", but in many clubs *keiko* starts with *rei-kirikaeshi* and ends with *kirikaeshi-rei* between *men-tsuke* (putting *men* on) and *men-tore* (taking *men* off).

Many highly-graded kendo instructors and authors of kendo books suggest that all of the fundamental elements of kendo can be learnt and refined through *kirikaeshi*. It includes repeated attacking sequences which help practitioners develop the transfer of power from the hips right through to the target. It develops correct *hasuji*, breathing, posture, *suri-ashi*, *fumikiri*, *fumikomi* and *taiatari*. Also, receiving big straight cuts and *sa-yū* (left-right) cuts while moving forwards and backwards builds important *motodachi* skills. *Kirikaeshi* is certainly an indispensable part of training. Regardless of your level, it should never be neglected.

Instructors should keep reminding their students, especially beginners, of the importance of *kirikaeshi* through explanation, demonstration and describing its relation and application to other exercises. Once initial competence has been achieved, I find that some students start to forget the significance of *kirikaeshi* and lose their motivation to practise it seriously. I have also encountered some students, both in Japan and overseas, who were never taught the objectives of practising *kirikaeshi* in the first place, and so simply think of it as a part of warming-up.

Explanations given by some instructors that *kirikaeshi* is important because you need it for gradings is also concerning. These comments may be the instructor's way of motivating their students, but the drawback is that those students might never fully appreciate the importance of it in relation to other exercises.

The developmental process of techniques in kendo is from "big, slow, and accurate" techniques to "big, quick, and accurate", and then to arrive at "small, quick, and accurate" techniques. In the case of *kirikaeshi*, practitioners should start practising with "big, slow, and accurate" cuts with the emphasis on correct *tachisuji* (striking path) and *hasuji* (blade angle).

I consider *kirikaeshi* to be an important basic exercise in the preparatory stage where practitioners build up their kendo foundation, and then make that stronger by incorporating the practice of *ashi-sabaki*, *suburi* and *kūkan-datosu*. It is important to move through these levels before progressing to "small, quick and accurate" techniques in *waza-geiko*. By this I mean that the techniques and movements of *kirikaeshi* are more closely related to those of *waza-geiko* than *ji-geiko* or *shiai*.

Incidentally most clubs seem to practise *waza-geiko* after practising *kirikaeshi*. The important thing is that students gradually develop their striking techniques with these three phases and not overlook the significance of *kirikaeshi*.

3. Uchikomi-geiko

I mentioned that *kirikaeshi* is followed by *waza-geiko* in many clubs, but I recommend that *uchikomi-geiko* be introduced before *waza-geiko*. According to the *Japanese-English Dictionary of Kendo* published by the All Japan Kendo Federation (2000, p. 106), *uchikomi-geiko* is, "a method of *keiko* in which one learns basic techniques of striking by responding to striking chances offered by *motodachi*." Through *uchikomi-geiko*, students can master "big, slow, and accurate" or "big, quick, and accurate" basic techniques not only for *men*, but also for *kote*, *dō* and *tsuki* attacks. Thus, *uchikomi-geiko* serves as further *keiko* in the preparatory stage before moving onto the "small, quick, and accurate" technical stage in subsequent *waza-geiko*.

Please remember that it is not only *kakarite* that benefits from *uchikomi-geiko*; it also allows *motodachi* the opportunity to learn important etiquette and attitudes required in the next stage of *waza-geiko*. I have outlined some methods of practising *uchikomi-geiko* below, and the various objectives and points to keep in mind while performing them.

Uchikomi-geiko is often done to improve stamina, but I suggest using it at this point to improve basic techniques, preferably with one *motodachi* to every three *kakarite* rather than practising in pairs. By doing this, the *kakarite* have more time to recover and are able to perform their best *uchikomi* each time. Each set should be about 15-20 seconds, and *motodachi* should change after receiving the *uchikomi* of three *kakarite*. Ideally, everyone should take turns at being *motodachi*, not just higher grades.

Kakarite should execute their *uchikomi* with "*100% ashi-sabaki - 100% posture - 100% accuracy - 50% speed*", keeping in mind that *uchikomi-geiko* is a vital preparatory stage on the road to "small, quick, and accurate". It is not easy to maintain good posture and make accurate cuts if you try to move and attack quickly, especially if you are a beginner. Speed can be increased gradually after students learn to control their *ashi-sabaki*, master their body movements, and acquire correct *shinai* handling.

Something interesting I have noticed is that even if I ask my students to do *uchikomi* at only 50% speed, most will practise at about 70%. To really practise at 50% speed, I have to ask them for 30%. There are various reasons for this. Perhaps they do not know what their 50% is, or maybe they have overestimated their own speed. Another reason might be that after watching senior students practising *uchikomi*, they feel that they have to move as fast as them.

As I mentioned, this kind of *uchikomi-geiko* is meant to be practised with *100% ashi-sabaki - 100% posture - 100% accuracy - 50% speed*. This does not mean that *kakarite* should strike softly. Even though it is only being performed at half-speed, *kakarite* should strike hard enough to warrant *ippon*.

Photo 1. *Men*

Photo 2. *Kote*

Photo 3. *Kote-men*
(Show *kote* and touch *men*
to signal the technique).

Photo 4. *Dō*

Photo 5. *Gyaku-dō*

Photo 6. *Tsuki*
(The left had touches *tsuki-
dare* quickly and returns to
the *tsuka*.)

Photo 7. *Taiatari*
(Show this before opening the target)
If *motodachi* wishes *kakarite* to do
hiki-waza after *taiatari*, they stand
fast. If *motodachi* wishes *kakarite*
perform further cuts going forward,
then *motodachi* moves backwards after *taiatari*.)

4. The Role of Motodachi

The *motodachi* has many things to think about and do in *uchikomi-geiko*. Learning how to be *motodachi* is at least as important as learning how to actually do the *uchikomi*; perhaps even more so. *Motodachi* have to offer each target clearly, and move in an appropriate manner taking into account the level, age and physique of *kakarite*. When partnered with a beginner, *motodachi* should encourage easier techniques such as *men*, *kote-men* and *dō*, and allow their partner to move though in a direct line after striking.

Intermediate level practitioners should attempt more advanced techniques such as *kote-dō* and *hiki-waza (men, kote* and *dō)* after performing *taiatari,* and experienced practitioners may try even more advanced techniques such as *gyaku-dō, tsuki* and *tsuki-men.* The photographs on the previous page show how to indicate which targets you wish *kakarite* to strike.

Here is an example of a not-so-helpful *motodachi*: *motodachi* receives *kakarite*'s strike and moves aside to allow them to pass through. *Motodachi* then waits for *kakarite* to come back to *issoku-ittō-no-maai* before offering the next target. This means that *kakarite* will stop moving momentarily. Even if *uchikomi-geiko* is performed slowly, it is important that *kakarite* keeps moving, and continually attacks without stopping.

The next target to strike should be visible to *kakarite* as soon as they turn around. *Motodachi* should follow *kakarite* through, and continually apply pressure, not just wait in the middle. This also keeps the exercise flowing. If *motodachi* is managing the distance properly, after *kakarite* turns around they should be at a distance where it takes only one *okuri-ashi* step with proper *fumikiri* and *fumikomi* to cut. It is not necessary to do *fumikiri* immediately after turning. Practising in this way means the *motodachi* provides *kakarite* with opportunities to improve their *hikitsuke* (pulling up the back foot).

Some highly-ranked instructors insist that practitioners should not step forwards using *okuri-ashi* after turning around and moving back in *uchikomi-geiko* or in *waza-geiko.* They recommend that the next attack should be launched immediately using *fumikiri* and *fumikomi.* This is technically and physically demanding, and is better suited to younger and more experienced practitioners. It may be very difficult for beginners or middle-aged and elderly practitioners. Maintaining proper posture and coordination between the upper and lower-body may not be possible, and injuries may occur due to over-exertion in this kind of practice. I would like to reiterate that *kakarite* should be focusing on proper *ashi-sabaki,* posture and accuracy, not on speed.

This kind of *uchikomi-geiko* can be practised by all members of a club regardless of differences in level and experience, provided that everyone understands how to be an effective *motodachi.* It is beneficial for all if practitioners learn the role of *motodachi* through *uchikomi-geiko* and become proficient in inciting and receiving effective attacks. This makes *waza-geiko* more satisfying, and leads to improved *ji-geiko* and *shiai. Waza-geiko* can then be an opportunity to focus on smaller, quicker and more complicated movements and techniques. Instructors also have the chance to focus on observing and instructing each *kakarite* on their *waza.*

5. Summary

Perhaps two of the most important things to be gained through *uchikomi-geiko* are the attitudes and etiquette that are necessary in kendo training. *Motodachi* must facilitate *kakarite*'s attack according to their level, age and physique and *kakarite* is also required to adjust their attacking strength and *taiatari* according to the same criteria. Thus, both attacker and receiver must cooperate for mutual benefit. Learning this attitude means you will be able to effectively train with a variety of different people. It is crucial that beginners appreciate this attitude, especially in clubs outside of Japan where practitioners of various different levels, experience and age often practice together. *Uchikomi-geiko* teaches us one of the most wonderful values in kendo: "Practitioners help each other, and develop together."

CHAPTER 5

WAZA-GEIKO

1. Introduction

In the previous chapter, I examined *kirikaeshi* and *uchikomi-geiko*, and methods for acquiring "big, slow, and accurate" cuts as a preparatory stage before moving on to the "'small, quick, and accurate" cuts of *waza-geiko*. I would like to reiterate an important point about *uchikomi-geiko*. In a kendo seminar that I ran in England in January 2006, I was demonstrating how to practise *uchikomi-geiko*. When the participants were about to start, one of them said "I can't do it." He explained, "Even if I do it at 50% speed, because of my age and condition I won't be able to move as quickly as the others." I replied to him, "This is not meant to be stamina or speed training; it's about building up your technique base. Your 50% pace does not have to be the same as someone elses, so don't compare yourself to others." He was reassured by this, and joined in the training. Although he was much slower than the others, it did not seem to matter to him anymore. He concentrated on his posture, *ashi-sabaki* and cutting, and finished the *uchikomi-geiko* with a feeling of satisfaction. If 50% is physically demanding, you can slow down or just act as *motodachi*; and if you are confident in your execution, you can go faster. Understanding the methodology and goals of practising *uchikomi-geiko* and in receiving as *motodachi* will enable a smooth progress on to *waza-geiko*.

In this chapter, I will examine *waza-geiko*. I do not intend to breakdown each technique or explain the specific *ashi-sabaki*, *shinai* handling, or timing each technique requires. Readers should already be familiar with the translated articles by Nakano Yasoji Sensei in "Nuts and Bolts" in *Kendo World*, and I urge you to consult this series to study the specific principles of each *waza*. My intention is to provide practitioners with suitable and effective methods for practising and teaching, as the training conditions and circumstances in Western countries are often different from those in Japan. I will discuss the important points behind each type of *keiko*, and outline how each *keiko* is interconnected. I will also present some methods for *waza-geiko*.

2. "Big, Slow, and Accurate" to "Small, Quick, and Accurate"

Practitioners should realise that tackling *waza-geiko* means starting to practise "small, quick, and accurate" cuts. This follows on after the "big, slow, and accurate", and then the "big, quick, and accurate" cuts employed while practising *ashi-sabaki, suburi, fumikiri, fumikomi, kirikaeshi* and *uchikomi*. Ideally, through *waza-geiko*, you should gradually develop your cutting action so that it becomes smaller, quicker and more practical, while always maintaining accuracy.

An especially important part of this process is the acquisition of correct *tenouchi*. According to the *Japanese-English Dictionary of Kendo* (All Japan Kendo Federation, 2000, p. 102), *tenouchi* refers to "the overall use of the hands when striking or responding, including the way of gripping the *shinai*, the tightening/loosening of the grip and the adjusting of the balance between the two hands." By acquiring correct *tenouchi*, we can attack and defend without relying too much on physical power, practise with anyone irrespective of difference in gender, age and physique, and continue to practise throughout our lives. It would not be an exaggeration to say that acquiring correct *tenouchi* is vital for lifelong kendo.

Most Japanese practitioners develop their *tenouchi* and *waza* through a great deal of physically demanding *keiko* in their younger years. Accordingly, how to teach and develop these skills in Western countries is a very important issue for both practitioners and instructors alike.

3. Requisite Teaching Skills

There are many instructors who can demonstrate *waza*, but often do not know how to explain and teach effectively, and are also unable to identify what their students may be doing wrong. *Waza-geiko* under the guidance of such instructors is usually carried out as follows: Firstly, they explain which *waza* will be practised. Next they demonstrate it, and then let their students try. They then walk around and sometimes give advice to a few students. Some students may be trying very hard, but may not be doing so well. The instructor is not exactly sure how to correct the problems or what advice they should give. In the end, due to time restrictions, or the fact that other students may be waiting, the instructor stops the practice and tries to encourage the students by saying that they will eventually be able to perform the *waza* correctly if they keep up the training. The problem is that this pattern often repeats itself with every different *waza* practice.

Two observations can be made from this example. First, the instructor lacks an understanding of *waza* and how it should be taught. Second, the instructor lacks the organisation and management skills required to teach *waza-geiko* to students of various levels. I will discuss these issues in more detail, and then present some methods for going through *waza-geiko*.

Everyone knows that we cannot learn a *waza* by merely watching it being performed, and then by trying it out ourselves a few times. Kendo is not that easy. The importance of repeated training in kendo is exemplified by the saying "*hyaku-ren-ji-toku*" (practising a hundred times makes the technique your own). However, repeating a *waza* without clearly understanding its purpose or the methodology of its practice is not effective. Instructors should fully understand the *waza* they are teaching, and have the necessary teaching skills to impart correct *ashi-sabaki*, body movement, *shinai* handling and so on before, during, and after *waza* execution.

Through correct and effective teaching methods, instructors allow their students to understand the significance of each *waza* and the purpose of each type of *keiko*. Students will then be motivated to practise even if they cannot execute the *waza* properly. Having all the students understand is a difficult task. It requires a lot of effort on the part of instructors to observe various teachers' methodologies, consult books and other sources of information, and incorporate these into their teaching repertoire.

Next, let us look at how an instructor's organisation and management skills influence the way in which *waza-geiko* is practised. In kendo clubs outside of Japan, it is most often the case that people of different levels and ages train together. Naturally, having everyone practise the same *waza* at the same pace is not effective because some will find it easier than others. Organising *waza-geiko* to suit everyone is often just as difficult as teaching the actual *waza,* sometimes even more so.

I always find myself nervous before teaching seminars because I do not know until the actual day how many people will be coming, and what disparity there will be in age and grade. I generally have to hurriedly alter my teaching plans on the spot after people turn up. I am conscious of the fact that many people may have come a long way to participate, and it is my sincere desire to teach and allow people to do *keiko* in a way which suits them.

Below, I have specified three different kinds of *waza-geiko* which I will describe how to teach and practise:

- *Waza-geiko* for building up *waza*
- *Waza-geiko* for developing and refining *waza*
- *Waza-geiko* for making techniques practical

4. Waza-geiko for Building up Waza

This is the first stage of *waza-geiko* that practitioners should tackle in order to build the foundations of their technique. This involves understanding the mechanism behind each movement that forms a *waza*, trying to execute each movement accurately, and then piecing each movement together to complete the whole technique. *Waza-geiko* at this level should be practised with "small, slow, and accurate" cuts; a progression from the "big, slow, and accurate" cuts of previous practices.

Practitioners begin by carefully observing their teacher's demonstrations, and trying to grasp each smaller movement of the whole. Then they attempt to perform each movement and the motion of the whole *waza* while referring to the advice of their teacher and seniors. Practitioners can stop and check each movement that they are performing, and can also start all over again whenever they need to. The entire practice can be performed as slowly as *kakarite* desires.

With simple *shikake-waza* (self-initiated attacks) such as *men*, *kote* and *kote-men*, practitioners will generally find it easy to develop proper form, and will be able to move on to the 'small, quick and accurate' stage. However, in the case of complicated *shikake-waza* and *ōji-waza*, it is advisable to take more time and work on understanding the mechanisms of each *waza* while building up proper form. At this stage, it is also imperative to develop correct *tenouchi* technique so that practitioners will not fall into the habit of striking in a way that relies solely on physical power and speed. Practitioners who have difficulty in doing *fumikiri* and *fumikomi* should also consider suitable ways to develop their *ashi-sabaki* at this stage.

I will now describe some points which are required of instructors in teaching this type of *waza-geiko*. As mentioned in the explanation of *uchikomi-geiko*, practitioners tend to move and attack more quickly than teachers advise; all the more so when other practitioners around them are moving and attacking quickly. In addition, when practitioners begin to work on small strikes using *tenouchi*, they often cannot make strong strikes, or produce nice striking sounds. They may become frustrated and start making larger and harder strikes to compensate, perhaps also feeling pressured by those around them who are performing the techniques well.

It is important that instructors remind students of the purpose of this stage of *waza-geiko* and correct these kinds of mistakes. Also, there is no need to specify how many times practitioners should try a particular *waza;* they should simply be provided with enough time to concentrate on building appropriate foundations with each technique at their own pace. Instructors should, however, create an atmosphere in which students feel comfortable, and can ask any questions that may arise.

5. Waza-geiko for Developing and Refining Waza

A *waza* follows the general sequence of "*kamae* → *seme-ai* → strike → *kime* → *zanshin*". As in the previous "*waza-geiko* for building up *waza*" stage, emphasis should be placed on understanding correct footwork, *shinai* handling, body movement, and on developing technique in the process. *Seme-ai* is not that important at this stage. What is important in the "*waza-geiko* for developing and refining *waza*" phase is that practitioners execute footwork, *shinai* handling, and body movements quickly, and try to make their actions automatic. Of course, this is something that should be refined over time.

When you practise *shikake-waza* (except *debana-waza* and *hiki-waza*) there will be some practitioners who have difficulty in executing strong *fumikiri* and *fumikomi* because of injury or age. I advise that they develop *waza* using their own individual movements while referring to the advice of their seniors and instructors. Furthermore, as I outlined in the explanation of *uchikomi-geiko*, you should not feel that you have to practise *waza* as fast as others. Instead, you should concentrate on performing *waza* at a speed that suits you.

When you practise *debana-waza* and *ōji-waza*, I recommend that you ask your partner to take a step in before striking. This way, you are given a clear signal when your partner is about to attack. As I also mentioned above, you should try to make your striking action "smaller, quicker, and accurate", but keep in mind that this should be a gradual process.

Another important factor in this stage of *waza-geiko* is *motodachi*'s attitude. *Motodachi*'s role is not simply just to receive *kakarite*'s attacks. For example, in the case of *shikake-waza*, creating an opening and passage for *kakarite* to go through, or else blocking with *taiatari*, is an important opportunity for *motodachi* to practise footwork. In *debana-waza* and *ōji-waza*, *motodachi* should be fully committed to the initial attack so that mutual benefit is gained from the practice.

I have seen many *motodachi* who simply stand still, do not maintain proper eye contact with *kakarite*, and attack off-centre so that *kakarite*'s strike will land on-target. This kind of *motodachi* misses many opportunities to further develop their own basic techniques, and simply wastes valuable *keiko* time. These actions are not helping *kakarite*.

Kakarite is only able to execute *shikake-waza* properly when *motodachi* shows full spirit, receives the attack properly, maintains proper eye contact, and quickly prepares for the next movement. *Kakarite* can only accomplish *debana-waza* and *ōji-waza* properly when *motodachi* commits to making direct attacks with proper technique. As long as these criteria are met, it does not matter if the attack itself is slow, or if some kind of signal is provided before the attack commences. Practitioners will not be able to help each other and improve without understanding these principles.

6. Waza-geiko for Making Waza Practical

At this stage, practitioners should try to execute all the elements of each *waza* (*kamae*, *seme-ai*, striking, *kime* and *zanshin*) in a practical fashion. Readying yourself after you have taken *kamae* is not practical; you should be physically and mentally ready to strike and to react to your opponent's attack when you take *kamae*.

I do not consider the expression, "kendo starts with *rei* and finishes with *rei*" as referring only to matters of etiquette. From the moment you face your opponent and bow, the fight has begun, and it is important to remain focused until the final *rei* with your opponent. In the *seme-ai* interval before striking, you should try to use various patterns of *seme*, footwork, *shinai* handling and body movement taking into consideration your partner's fighting style.

An important element of striking is "*kime*". According to the *Japanese-English Dictionary of*

Kendo (All Japan Kendo Federation, 2000, p. 50), *kime* is defined as "the techniques that make a strike valid" and "the action of gripping the *shinai* when striking." Here I am referring to the former. After a strike, you must complete your attack by positioning yourself to avoid any counterattack, and also in a manner in which your *zanshin* will not be disturbed. Generally you either move away from, or close in towards your opponent, giving the message to your opponent, the *shinpan*, or the grading panellists that you got the point clearly.

Kime is one of the components of movement that make your strike an *ippon* in conjunction with *ki*, *ken* and *tai* (spirit, sword, and body). As explained in Chapter 2, we often use the word 'cut' to describe a strike in kendo, and we learn to strike with a feeling of cutting using correct *hasuji*, even though we are just using a *shinai*. Here, I would also like to introduce another idea of what a 'cut' is which is more advanced. I often explain that even if your *shinai* lands on the target, it is just a 'hit' unless you have *kime*.

$$\text{Kamae} \rightarrow \text{Seme-ai} \rightarrow \text{Hit} \rightarrow \text{Kime} \rightarrow \text{Zanshin}$$
$$\diagdown \quad \diagup$$
$$\text{Cut}$$

At this stage of *waza-geiko*, when you miss striking a target or your attack is poorly timed, you should attack again immediately. If you miss again, you should keep attacking until you get a successful *ippon*. By approaching *waza-geiko* in this way, you will eventually become able to judge immediately and intuitively whether you need to apply *kime* and display *zanshin* to secure a successful point, or whether you need to attack again. In *ji-geiko* and *shiai* I often see practitioners make a successful 'hit', but then continue to make further attacks without using *kime*. After refereeing a *shiai* many people also ask me, "Why didn't you award an *ippon* there?" Remember that an *ippon* is not something you are given, but is something you have to win for yourself.

Kime should flow naturally into *zanshin* so that you are physically and mentally ready for the opponent's next possible movement. Try to eliminate the gap between the *zanshin*, *kamae*, and *seme-ai* for your next *waza*; all of these processes should overlap. For example, if each partner is practising a *waza* four times, then neither should take a break, nor relax even momentarily until both sides have completed the *waza* four times. This is a good example of maintaining proper *en* with your partner.

To help understand *en*, consider a beginner's *ji-geiko*, *shiai* or *shinsa*; most move through after attacking and turn their back on their opponent regardless of whether the strike was successful or not. This happens because they are trying to do the same thing that they do in *waza-geiko*. They are under the misconception that moving through after a strike, and then turning around and taking *kamae* is necessary to complete a *waza*. Eye contact and connection with the opponent is lost with each attack. One of the main objectives with beginners' *keiko* is that they learn to have greater control. Although it is quite natural for beginners to attack this way, as they gain experience they need to be able to maintain a connection with their opponent to be ready to attack at any time. At this stage of *waza-geiko*, I advise that you consider this concept of *en*, and try to apply it in your training.

7. Consolidating the Three Types of Waza-geiko

So far I have only explained how to perform these three types of *waza-geiko* on their own. The process of learning a technique does not always follow the logical order described in Figure 1. For example, let us say that you move on to the "*waza-geiko* for developing and refining *waza*" phase and started practising at a faster speed. After a while you realise that the footwork you learned in the previous stage of *waza-geiko* is not actually suitable for faster movements. In this case, you may need to go back to the previous stage and modify your footwork.

As another example, let us say that you moved on to the "*waza-geiko* for making *waza* practical" phase, and tried practising *waza* at high speed utilising *seme* and *kime*. After a while you realise that you have picked up bad habit of relying too much on your right hand when you perform *suriage-men*. In this case, you may need to go back to the previous stage (or even the first of the three stages) to correct the problem.

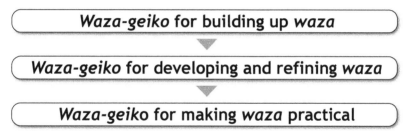

Figure 1

Occasionally when we concentrate a lot on practising a particular *waza*, we sometimes neglect to review other *waza* that we may have been proficient at before. As Figure 2 shows, *waza-geiko* can move back and forth between the different stages.

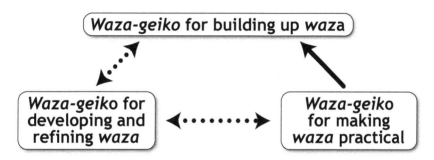

Figure 2

8. Summary

By applying this principle to *waza-geiko*, instructors can organise training sessions where each member can perform *waza* at a stage appropriate for them. For example, students can be divided into three groups according to level and experience, and they can practise the same *waza* at their respective stages (Figure 1). Even if they are not divided into groups, they can tell each other at what stage they want to practise the *waza*, and how they want their partner to attack or receive (Figure 2). Naturally, communication between club members is quite important in this case. It is also possible to have students practise different *waza* while they are divided into groups, or even practise different stages. Instructors need to ensure that students have a clear understanding of the purpose of each stage of *waza-geiko*, and should encourage them to practise at a stage that is appropriate to their level, regardless of the manner in which the *keiko* is organised.

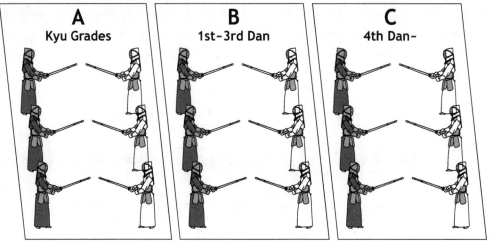

Figure 1: *Waza-geiko* in groups according to levels and experience

Figure 2:
Waza-geiko in groups with communication

CHAPTER 6

KAKARI-GEIKO

1. Introduction

In this chapter I will discuss *kakari-geiko*. Many high-ranking instructors tell us how important *kakari-geiko* is for improvement in kendo, and I assume the majority of practitioners already know this. I would also make the assumption that *kakari-geiko* is the least popular component of kendo training. Many practitioners negatively think of *kakari-geiko* as "hard and exhausting" hoping to finish it quickly, or avoid it altogether.

Kakari-geiko is often used as penalty-*keiko* for somebody who comes late to training, or who causes problems for the club in some way. It is also used as 'special birthday training' or to farewell someone who is leaving the club. When I was in university, one of my friends in the kendo club overslept on the morning we were about to leave for a training camp. In his panic to get to the train station on time he completely forgot to bring his *bōgu*. That evening, our club captain gave him a SUPER SPECIAL KAKARI-GEIKO session. The whole club also looked forward to respectfully giving an EVIL KAKARI-GEIKO present to our club instructor each year on his birthday to thank him for his hard work.

I will discuss the purpose of *kakari-geiko*, and introduce some types of *kakari-geiko* useful for developing certain technical aspects of kendo, while taking into account the differing circumstances of training in Western countries.

2. The Purpose of Kakari-geiko

According to the *Japanese-English Dictionary of Kendo* (AJKF, 2000, p. 42), *kakari-geiko* is defined as "The *keiko* method where the trainee for a short period practises striking the *motodachi* with all his/her might, using all the *waza* he /she has learned, and without thinking of being struck and dodged." What should to be considered here is the difference between *kakari-geiko* and *uchikomi-geiko*.

Uchikomi-geiko is a method of *keiko* for the acquisition of basic techniques where practitioners continuously attempt to strike or thrust at the targets provided by the *motodachi*. It does not necessarily have to be done at a fast pace, but emphasis should be placed on big and accurate cuts even if performed at a slow pace. On the other hand, *kakari-geiko* requires small, quick, and sharp cuts. "Accurate" cuts should also be attempted, but the reason I have not mentioned them here is because *motodachi* will sometimes dodge, block or counterattack in *kakari-geiko*. Through *kakari-geiko*, *kakarite* should aim to improve their *ashi-sabaki*, *shinai* handling, physical speed, *tenouchi*, *fumikiri*, *fumikomi*, coordination, technique combinations, stamina, fighting spirit, and mental strength. However individual instructors or *motodachi* may choose to focus on differing aspects. This will affect how long and how many times *kakari-geiko* is practised, how often *motodachi* lets *kakarite* go through, and whether *motodachi* receives *kakarite*'s attack with *taiatari*, dodges, blocks or counterattacks.

3. Motodachi in Kakari-geiko

As mentioned in the above explanation of *kakari-geiko*, *motodachi* receives *kakarite*'s *kakari-geiko* and plays the role of instructor in order to develop and improve *kakarite*'s techniques, as well as physical and mental strength. In clubs in Japan there are often enough seniors, *sensei*, or at least enough practitioners of the same level to act as *motodachi*. However, in kendo clubs in Western countries, practitioners of different levels, experience, and age often train together meaning that even juniors may have to act as *motodachi* and receive *kakari-geiko*.

Just as in other kinds of *keiko*, *motodachi* in *kakari-geiko* must ensure that things run smoothly, and that *kakarite* benefits from the practice. When you act as *motodachi* you must keep in mind that it is your role to develop and improve *kakarite*'s kendo, even if *kakarite* is senior to you. If everyone realises this, and can perform the role of *motodachi* properly, then everybody will enjoy practising together, and will be able to help each other develop and improve regardless of differences in level, experience and age.

Although *motodachi* plays an important role in *kakarite*'s kendo development, this does not mean that *kakari-geiko* is only intended to benefit *kakarite*. I would like to stress that if *motodachi* has an appropriate attitude and performs *kakari-geiko* properly, then they can also glean many benefits from the exercise. Practitioners should learn to appreciate the effectiveness of *kakari-geiko* and how important it is to improve kendo skills through mutual cooperation. Keeping this in mind, I will now introduce some types of *kakari-geiko* which are intended to benefit *motodachi* just as much as *kakarite*.

4. Fifty-Fifty Kakari-geiko

In "50-50 *kakari-geiko*", *motodachi* receives 50% of the *kakarite*'s techniques, and counterattacks against the other 50%. There are two ways to act as *motodachi* in this exercise. The first is to clearly offer targets or yell out where *kakarite* should attack, as in *uchikomi-geiko*. The second is to hold *kamae* and have *kakarite* attempt to break it. When counterattacking, *motodachi* does not need to move through after their strike; they should strike with one step. Wherever *motodachi* steps, it is important for them to keep facing *kakarite*, and to keep *kakarite* moving and attacking in a good rhythm with continuous *en*.

Obviously, through this type of *kakari-geiko*, *motodachi* can improve their *ashi-sabaki*, body movement, striking speed, timing, and *tenouchi* against *kakarite*'s fast attacks. Practising in this way is intended to benefit both *motodachi* and *kakarite*, but *motodachi* must judge several things simultaneously in order to achieve this – something that is easier said than done. A less experienced practitioner receiving very fast *kakari-geiko* may not be able to keep up with the rapidly changing scenarios of the 50-50 format. This may result in awkward counterattacking on the part of *motodachi*, and *kakarite* may not be able to attack smoothly or with a suitable rhythm. If *kakari-geiko* like this proves to be frustrating, then simply alter the ratio of receiving and counterattacking to 70-30, or 80-20, or only attempt counterattacks when you feel more confident as *motodachi*.

5. Defensive Kakari-geiko

In "Defensive *kakari-geiko*", *motodachi* attempts to defend all attacks by *kakarite* whilst *kakarite* attempts to break *motodachi*'s defences and strike successfully. Strangely enough, in kendo, there is little opportunity to learn defensive techniques compared to other sports or activities. Practitioners often devise defences based on their own training experiences. The kendo expression "*bōgyo no tame no bōgyo nashi*" means "no defence for the sake of defence". This is meant to encourage attacking techniques that ultimately also serve as a form of defence; a habit we need to develop in our training.

I suspect that a considerable number of instructors take this idea too literally and never teach defensive techniques at all. Many practitioners, especially beginners, then try to defend against attacks in their own inefficient ways, missing opportunities to learn from the concept of "*bōgyo no tame no bōgyo nashi*."

Okajima (1992) points out that beginners' anxiety and fear of their opponents' attacks prevent them from finding opportunities for a strike. I would suggest therefore that instructors teach basic defensive techniques to beginners before they begin practising *ji-geiko*. I do not mean simply blocking *shinai* against *shinai* however. Beginners should be taught correct *metsuke* (positioning of the eyes) and how to defend through the application of *ki-ken-tai-no-itchi*.

Beginners tend to gaze mainly at their opponent's *shinai*, which generally results in them moving their hands in response to their opponent's *shinai* movement. This also means they are often easily caught out by feinting actions such as a *dō* strike that starts out as an exaggerated *men* strike. According to the *Japanese-English Dictionary of Kendo* (2000, p. 62), "*metsuke*" is defined as "The act of paying attention to the opponent's whole body while looking into his/her eyes." The term "*enzan-no-metsuke* (looking at a far-away mountain)" also provides us with clues on how to focus our vision when confronting an opponent. "It is important to look at the figure of the opponent as a whole rather than at a particular point, as if looking at a far-away mountain." (p. 24)

In order to defend by applying *ki-ken-tai-no-itchi*, one needs to keep a positive frame of mind, something which extends to *shinai* handling, footwork and body movement. The expression *ki-ken-tai-no-itchi* is normally associated with striking actions, but it also relates to defence, something beginners will experience difficulty with. Even though the defensive postures and techniques that beginners learn may not prove effective for them in the short term, it is important that they persist and develop these through the experience of being repeatedly attacked. In the long term, practitioners will be able to develop more efficient defensive tactics to suit themselves.

Okajima (1992) argues that strong defence is an important element of performance in kendo. From this we can assume that learning defensive techniques with an understanding of "*bōgyo no tame no bōgyo nashi*" will be quite useful towards helping us execute higher level tactics in the future. In "Defensive *kakari-geiko*", *motodachi* is given the opportunity to improve their defensive skills, and *kakarite* learns how to outwit their opponent, and how to break their opponent's guard in speedy and rapidly changing situations.

6. Mutual Kakari-geiko

In "Mutual *kakari-geiko*", both practitioners act as *kakarite* and attempt to strike each other at the same time. Both need to strike continuously without pause. This does not mean the attacks should be frenzied or random; each *kakarite* should try to launch and carry through with their attack before their partner can react, or alternatively anticipate their partner's intentions and make an appropriate counterattack. Sometimes you may be practising this with someone who has more experience, someone who is faster or has a wider repertoire of *waza*, but you should not let this make you afraid of being struck or countered. Regardless of how your partner reacts, you should not stop once you begin to launch your attack.

For example, if your partner attempts *men-nuki-dō* against your *men* attack, you should not stop halfway through and try to protect your *dō*. Since both sides are acting as *kakarite*, attacking and counterattacking should be the main focus of the exercise. Put everything into each attack without thinking about possible outcomes, and use different *waza* depending on how you interpret your partner's intentions. Do not fall into the trap of getting too carried away with competitive flourish during technique execution; you must focus on maintaining good posture and striking firmly. Otherwise you may start ignoring proper *maai*, or begin using incorrect *hasuji* when striking.

7. Summary

I introduced three different types of *kakari-geiko* along with some important points for consideration. In conclusion, I would add that if you have difficulty in practising *kakari-geiko* as *kakarite* at a fast pace due to age or injury, then it is completely acceptable to perform it at a slower pace, or with limited motion. If this proves difficult, then you can simply act as *motodachi*. There are many practitioners who mistakenly think that *kakari-geiko* is only intended for young and fit practitioners. However it is an important exercise in which everyone can participate, and through which both *motodachi* and *kakarite* can improve their techniques by modifying the training to suit their own purposes. I hope everyone will practise and learn to enjoy *kakari-geiko* with all the members of their club.

CHAPTER 7

JI-GEIKO

1. Introduction

Sparring practice against an opponent is called *ji-geiko* and it forms the core of all types of *keiko* in kendo. During *ji-geiko* the practitioner can try out various *waza* against a partner in a more realistic manner than *kihon-geiko* (the practice of basics which includes *waza-geiko*) where various technical elements are repeated in a rehearsed manner under relatively controlled circumstances. Through free sparring, we learn and improve our methods of *seme* (pressure and attack), and also how we react to the *seme* of our opponent.

Ji-geiko allows us to identify our strengths and weaknesses so that we know what to focus on the next time we perform *kihon-geiko*. It is a chance to progress on a technical and psychological level. If we simply approach *ji-geiko* as a contest in which the goal is to beat our opponent, then we will not truly develop as *kendō-ka*. It is important therefore, that we perform *ji-geiko* with a correct understanding of its objectives. The purpose of this chapter is to examine the role of *ji-geiko*, and present some training ideas for *kendō-ka* to apply in future practices. Firstly we will investigate the relationships between *kihon-geiko*, *kata-geiko* (the practice of forms), and *ji-geiko*.

2. The Relationship between Kihon-geiko, Kata-geiko and Ji-geiko

Besides *ji-geiko,* the other two main elements of training in kendo are *kihon-geiko,* and *kata-geiko. Kihon-geiko* entails practicing the same technique repeatedly in a rehearsed manner so that we become proficient in its use and develop full *kiai* (spirit), good posture and *ki-ken-tai-no-itchi* (union of spirit, sword and body). *Kata-geiko,* on the other hand, places more emphasis on sword handling than *kihon-geiko* as a wooden sword called a *bokutō* is used instead of a bamboo *shinai.* An often overlooked fact regarding *kata-geiko* is that it also teaches us how to breathe from the abdomen.

Although *kihon-geiko, kata-geiko* and *ji-geiko* are all performed separately, they are all fundamentally connected. Despite this connection, there are some practitioners who can perform *kihon-geiko* and *kata-geiko* well, but whose *ji-geiko* is unsightly due to a lack of upper and lower-body coordination. If these individuals are setting themselves gradual tasks for improvement, then there is no major need for concern. However, another problem lies with those who simply want to beat their opponent, or rain down as many random blows on them as possible. This kind of attitude towards *ji-geiko* demonstrates a concern with only short-term goals and immediate gratification.

There are others who take the opposite extreme to this and focus on their posture and form with little regard for control of centre (*chūshin*) through the mutual interplay of pressuring and attacking (*seme-ai*). If these individuals do this knowingly in order to make particular improvements to their kendo, then once again there is no major cause for concern; however if it becomes a habit, I feel it degrades the *ji-geiko* experience, and robs us of its true benefits.

3. Methods to Fully Benefit from Ji-geiko

Although it is a natural tendency, practitioners should not favour one kind of *keiko* over another; *kihon-geiko, kata-geiko* and *ji-geiko* are all equally important. *Ji-geiko* is a chance to practise what we learned during *kihon-geiko* and *kata-geiko* and vice-versa. If we recognise this, then the whole experience is enriched and we will enjoy all three types of *keiko.* As mentioned previously, one objective of *ji-geiko* is to identify our strengths and weaknesses under less restrictions than are imposed by *kihon-geiko.* In addition to this, Tomiki (1991) states that another purpose of *ji-geiko* in modern kendo is that it allows practitioners to grasp the austere spiritual aspects of kendo as a form of *budō.* Centuries ago, martial artists often engaged in duels or fought in battles to test their abilities. In modern times the life-and-death element has been removed, and the sportification of *bujutsu* arts facilitated the introduction of rules and protective armour for safety.

The modern practitioner of kendo is expected to control his or her emotions when in competition against an opponent, and this battle of emotions is most evident in *ji-geiko.* Poor emotional control in competition often stems from misguided attitudes towards *ji-geiko*; it is vital that everyone understands this fact. Approaches vary from person to person but there are important guidelines that beginners and more experienced practitioners can respectively follow. The personal goals that a person sets, and also the types of opponent they face dictate how they perform *ji-geiko.* Types of opponents may include beginners, seniors, opposite sex, or the elderly.

4. Ji-geiko for Kyū Grade Holders

Practitioners at this level should try to employ mainly *shikake-waza*. This does not mean simply striking *men* and *kote* only, but using all of the applicable *waza* that you have learned in *kihon-geiko* and *kata-geiko* without being afraid of losing or performing the *waza* poorly. By striking in this way, you will come to better understand the most effective timing and distancing for each *waza*. At this stage you should keep trying to attack using your own initiative.

Another important point is that you should not stop your movement after striking, but try to complete your attack and quickly prepare yourself for the next action. In *ji-geiko* beginners often lose their concentration and readiness as soon as they finish their first attack, and then they move back awkwardly to the position they started from. It is important to always maintain concentration wherever you are, and to prepare for the next action as soon as you have finished your first attack.

Generally, most beginners are not taught how to defend against attacks and so, quite often, they may simply be facing their opponent absentmindedly with tense shoulders, and may even shut their eyes from time to time. They may back off, or jump away from an opponent's attack if they do not manage to launch an attack first themselves. Naturally, this can be caused by fear of being attacked, but it can make a big difference if beginners are taught the significance of *kōbō-itchi* and *kentai-itchi*. These terms collectively refer to "combining motions of attack and defence into one".

In kendo terms they are defined as, "Always being mentally and physically ready to defend against the opponent's counterattack while attacking, and ready to counterattack while defending" (*Japanese-English Dictionary of Kendo*, p. 47). In other words, a defensive action should not just be performed for the sake of defence, but should flow into the next attack, or allow a counterattack.

An ideal defence does not glue the practitioner to the spot or lock their hands in a blocking position; the knees should be relaxed allowing smooth footwork and *shinai* control. With time and experience you will learn more complex methods of combined attack-defence. Practitioners at this level must make large body movements, and not simply try to strike their opponent more times than they themselves have been hit. It takes a long time to rid oneself of bad habits developed in attack and defence at this stage. Follow the advice of your *senpai* and *sensei* and apply it in your next *ji-geiko* session.

5. Ji-geiko for Shodan to 3-dan Grade Holders

Practitioners at this level are required to further refine their *shikake-waza* and also focus on the use of *hiki-waza* (techniques performed while moving backwards). Attacks should be performed in complete motions and, as mentioned previously, winning and losing should not be the main concern. The tally of successful points that you and your opponent have taken is not important; what is significant is how and why each strike was successful. An attitude of "*utte-hansei, utarete-kansha*" (reflect when you strike successfully, and be grateful when you are struck) is a sign of a mature kendo practitioner; this means that the practitioner is able to evaluate their own successful attacks, and appreciates the lesson they are taught when successfully struck by their opponent.

The next stage is to be aware of and develop *san-sappō* (the three ways to overwhelm an opponent). The first is to overwhelm the opponent's *ki* (spirit) with the fullness of your own *ki*. The next is to 'kill' the opponent's *ken* (sword) by pressuring or deflecting with your own. The third and last way is to thwart the *waza* (technique) execution of your opponent. First to third *dan* grade holders are permitted to rely more on the *ken* and *waza* components of *san-sappō* than on *ki*, because it is still too early for them to perform the kendo that utilises *ki* and power of presence that 6-*dan* and 7-*dan* grade holders are capable of.

First to third *dan* grade holders should use a variety of *waza* in *ji-geiko* employing dynamic *shinai* control, body movement and footwork. The approximate ratio of *shikake-waza* to *ōji-waza* should be 4:1. It is important to keep in mind that when performing advanced level *ōji-waza* you should not wait for your opponent to attack before responding, as you will usually be too late; you need to actually lure your opponent into making the attack you desire. Many people worry that they cannot perform *ōji-waza* well due to inappropriate movement or form when the problem actually lies in them not luring their opponent into attack. At this level, *ōji-waza* are still very calculated sets of movements, and they are not expected to be as instinctive as they are to higher grade holders.

6. Ji-geiko for 4-dan and 5-dan

Practitioners who reach these relatively high grades are generally *senpai* or *sensei* to the lower grades, and at this level they are expected to have developed the ability to read their opponent's actions and intentions. You should be able to handle yourself well in a wide variety of situations, be decisive and instinctive in your actions, and be able to control your opponent's centre with small *shinai* and body movements by interpreting their intentions. Your attacks should generally follow this control of centre and be performed with an economy of *shinai* and body motion.

This does not mean that once you reach 4-*dan* you should immediately restrain your motions in an attempt to make them as minimal as possible. The changes should occur gradually and start with you moving the focus of your kendo away from physicality and more towards controlling your opponent through your mental state and application of *ki*. At this level, the recommended ratio of *shikake-waza* to *ōji-waza* should be 3:2.

It is important to maintain an upright posture so that you can move in any direction smoothly, and the back of your left knee (*hikagami*) should have enough tension that you can push off quickly. If you try to apply this, but find that your left leg is cramping, it means that you were not using your leg correctly in the first place. If you start to experience this cramping, you are now using your leg in the correct way.

Those at 4-*dan* or 5-*dan* level must not be embarrassed when struck; our kendo can be improved by being struck by an opponent no matter how high our grade. Even though small and economical movements are preferred at this level, you should not hesitate to use larger *waza* when you see an opportunity. Some practitioners prefer to use one kind of technique such as *men*, but it is still important to apply a wide range of *waza*.

This also applies to attacks from *tsubazeriai*. Some highly-graded practitioners fall into the habit of dropping their level of concentration once in *tsubazeriai* (the position when two opponents are close enough to each other that their *shinai* lock together near the *tsuba* hand-guards). Even in this position, you must always maintain concentration, and be prepared to attack whenever the chance arises.

7. Ji-geiko for 6-dan

To describe how *ji-geiko* at this level should be, I will refer to a book entitled *Kendō Nendai-betsu Keiko-hō - Michi-no-Kaori* (Age-Appropriate Kendo Training Methods, 2000) written by kendo teacher Sumi Masatake, Hanshi 8-*dan*. Sumi points out that practitioners at this level should be modest, not arrogant, and still have a desire to improve themselves despite having reached this high grade.

In *ji-geiko*, their *shinai* control and body motion should be refined to an even higher level of economy and rationality than before. Practitioners who have reached this grade are usually middle-aged or older, which means that their physical abilities have declined somewhat since their athletic prime. Accordingly, this decline can be compensated for with further refinement of *ki* and *waza*.

Sumi (2000) also points out that practitioners at this level should begin to shift the focus of their kendo more towards *debana-waza* (attacking at the moment the opponent is about to attack). He also encourages techniques such as *suriage-waza* (rising deflections) that use sideways or diagonal *tai-sabaki* (body movement). At this level it is more important to be able to read your opponent's movements and intentions and in reacting appropriately.

To become proficient at *debana-waza*, Sumi advises that the best course of action is to practise for yourself at your own timing as there are seldom people of higher rank to be able to seek advice from. Practitioners should therefore experiment with how to best upset their opponent's balance, and how to lure their opponents into making an attack to perform the *debana-waza*. The *hansei* or reflection process after *ji-geiko* should become more involved, and all factors should be considered, i.e. attack, defence and counterattack.

Another suggestion by Sumi is that the practitioner chooses one target to strike, and one *waza* to strike it with in *ji-geiko*, regardless of how their opponent chooses to attack. This narrow focus allows the practitioner to quickly discover the ideal timing for each type of *debana-waza* they wish to develop. He also explains that there are many details for practitioners at this level to consider, such as how to improve *kamae* (stance), how to better keep balance, how to tense and relax various muscles, how to breathe, and what type of *shinai* to choose (p. 202).

Sumi confirms the connection between *kihon-geiko*, *kata-geiko* and *ji-geiko*, and acknowledges that kendo is a path of *shugyō* (austere training) that must be followed throughout one's whole life. There are no shortcuts along its way, and so *kihon-geiko* and *kata-geiko* should not be neglected, even by those practitioners 6-*dan* and above. Even at these levels, practitioners should follow the guidelines as outlined for *kyū* grades, i.e. try to apply *waza* in *ji-geiko* as you have practised them in *kihon-geiko* and *kata-geiko*.

8. Summary

This chapter was concerned largely with the connection between *kihon-geiko*, *kata-geiko* and *ji-geiko*. In the next chapter I will discuss how to approach *ji-geiko* with opponents of differing ages, gender, and skill levels.

CHAPTER 8

THE RIGHT ATTITUDE IN JI-GEIKO

1. Introduction

In the previous chapter I outlined the connections between *ji-geiko*, *kihon-geiko* and *kata-geiko*, and examined various methods of approaching *ji-geiko* for practitioners at elementary, intermediate and advanced levels. In this chapter I will discuss how practitioners should tackle *ji-geiko* with different types of opponents, focusing on strategies for sparring against someone of higher level, similar level, or junior level, of the opposite gender, or of senior age.

2. Ji-geiko Against Senior Levels

It should be mentioned from the outset that you should try to get the *shodachi* (first cut), no matter who you are engaging in *ji-geiko* with. Until a clean point is taken, *ji-geiko* should be played out as an earnest *ippon-shōbu* irrespective of differences in grade and experience. If you were duelling with real swords there would be no second chance, and it is important to appreciate this notion and take the encounter seriously. This mind-set differentiates kendo from other sports, and affords kendo its *budō* status.

After the initial *shodachi* you should then focus on *shikake-waza*, but avoid attacking haphazardly against seniors. Practitioners of 1-*kyū* or 1-*dan* level should work on breaking the senior's *chūshin* through footwork, *shinai* and body movement. You must not be afraid of being dodged or counterattacked, and should complete all of your attacks without stopping mid-way through your motions.

When a senior successfully scores *debana-waza* or *ōji-waza* techniques against you, it is an opportunity to develop and modify your *shikake-waza*. If you simply wait for the senior to attack you then you gain nothing from the experience. You should use your entire repertoire of techniques and give everything you have to the encounter. Sumi (2000) advises that juniors should focus only on *shikake-waza* and that when performing *ji-geiko* against a senior, they should aim to perform at a tempo in which they will physically tire out over the course of approximately 5 minutes.

Those of 2-*dan*, 3-*dan* and 4-*dan* rank should focus on methods of dominating *chūshin* with less emphasis on footwork and *shinai* movement. Even at this level practitioners should never be afraid of the senior's counterattacks, and should make full and complete striking motions. In summary, no matter what your grade, if you are practising against a senior, then you should focus on the use and refinement of *shikake-waza*. By reflecting on the experience you will be able to analyse how effective or ineffective your *seme* is and know what to focus on in the next training session.

3. Ji-geiko Against Junior Levels

When practising against someone of a junior level it is still important to try to take *shodachi* with complete concentration, however, after *shodachi* is made, the aim of *ji-geiko* should not be to simply beat them. It is selfish to obtain satisfaction through making short work of a junior, and you should avoid falling into this habit for both their sake and your own. There is a tendency to want to show off to those watching, and impress them with how easily you beat your opponent, but such vanity should be admonished.

Seniors have a responsibility to develop juniors' skills by allowing them to develop their strengths and identify their weaknesses. This means striking the junior when there is an opening, but also allowing them to strike you occasionally. This type of *keiko* is called *hikitate-geiko*, and is possibly one of the most difficult kinds of *keiko* to perform properly. Juniors will lose enthusiasm and motivation if seniors just make short work of them all the time, but the same negative result occurs if the senior makes blatant openings for the junior to strike.

Here, the senior walks a fine line and I recommend that the senior might even need to downplay his or her skills and face the junior as if they are just a fraction better than them, perhaps half a *dan* rank higher for the sake of comparison. Even in these cases, the senior must be fully engaged in the encounter, and not let their guard or concentration waver.

So when should a senior attack, perform a counterattack, or allow an attack? Seniors should attack when there is an obvious opening on the junior's part to show them their mistake. Seniors should counterattack when the junior launches into an attack without strong *seme*. Seniors should allow an attack to be completed successfully against them when the junior shows good *seme* and choice of timing and opportunity. *Hikitate-geiko* is an excellent opportunity to demonstrate to juniors the appropriate opportunities to make a strike. Seniors are expected to make juniors understand the importance of maintaining concentration and keeping *en*. Seniors can take the opportunity to cut if the junior is careless after their attack.

There is a well-known saying that "Everyone is my teacher" (*Ware igai mina shi nari*), implying that everyone has something they can teach us, even if they are of a lower level. This is how seniors should approach *ji-geiko* with juniors. A common misconception that we hear is: "I have the highest rank in the *dōjō*, so there's nobody I can learn from." This is certainly not the case, and is only dependant on your mind-set.

Much can be learned from *ji-geiko* against lower grades. If you are confident that you can beat a junior, then why not set yourself a goal to work on, or give yourself a handicap to make things interesting? For example, you could focus on attacking *men*, taking into account specific ideas such as what distance to cut from and how to make the opportunity. In this way, practising with a specific idea in mind will be more productive than cutting with the same pattern over and over. The practice of applying a handicap to yourself will also teach you how to perform under more ad verse conditions. Another example might be trying to fence from *chika-ma* against a smaller opponent, or focusing on *debana-waza* opportunities by luring your opponent into making an attack under pressure. I reiterate the importance for seniors of not falling into a point-scoring match mentality with juniors, or beating them for self-satisfaction.

4. Ji-geiko Against Someone of the Same Level

Sparring against someone of the same or similar level provides you with the opportunity to reflect on your progress. This experience is enhanced if your opponent is of similar age and experience level. It is important to perform *ji-geiko* against an opponent like this whenever possible. People tend to avoid competing with their rivals, but this is not a productive attitude to have in kendo. Many practitioners also feel the urge to retaliate and win back face quickly when they are struck by their opponent, which can lead to a lack of proper *seme*. This desire to win back the point must be repressed, and the practitioner should instead focus on taking *chūshin*.

Through *ji-geiko* with people of the same level you can examine the *seme* and *waza* which worked against juniors in a new light, and gauge their effectiveness by a different standard. In doing so, you can see if your rival training partners have strengths that you do not, and vice-versa. Despite this one-upmanship, it is still important that you treat your rivals with the respect they deserve as training partners, and cooperate with each other for mutual improvement. This is an important aspect of *shugyō* in kendo.

5. Ji-geiko Against Someone of Senior Age

I will now examine the scenario of advanced age rather than advanced skill, i.e. someone who is of senior age as opposed to senior grade. You must completely refrain from performing powerful *taiatari* and *tsuki* techniques against elderly people in *ji-geiko* as they may have less physical body weight or strength than yourself. In general, you should avoid *seme*, *waza* and all physical contact that mainly relies on physical strength.

However, this does not mean you should perform weak kendo; you should still make complete attacks and maintain a high level of pressure. The only concessions you should make are in physical *taiatari* collisions and the reduction in your applied power. If you dismiss *ji-geiko* with an older practitioner as non-beneficial then that will prove to be the case; it all depends on your perspective. Elderly practitioners may not use as many types of *waza* powerfully or quickly, but they often have a brilliant ability to read their opponent's intentions and movements. They are role-models who can demonstrate to younger practitioners how they can modify their kendo to enjoy practice when they get older.

6. Ji-geiko for a Male Practitioner Facing a Female Opponent

When facing a female opponent, a male practitioner should refrain from using *taiatari* and *waza* that rely too much on physical power. He should also not become overly obsessed with not being struck, and should not become frustrated when they cannot strike as he wishes. If you fall into these traps then you may start striking haphazardly in an attempt to be the first to score.

When you ignore differences in gender, height and physique, then you demonstrate a lack of respect for your opponent, and this is the worst type of kendo. Even if you win convincingly in this manner, there would have been no quality connection between you and your opponent, and nobody stands to gain anything from the experience. Your opponent in *ji-geiko* is not an enemy to destroy; rather, you and your opponent are partners helping each other towards a mutual goal of self-improvement.

If you are much taller than your female opponent, you should use this as an opportunity to practise fencing from *chika-ma*. You may feel cramped or crowded by your opponent, but being able to practise in *chika-ma* without relying on brute strength is an important skill. If your female opponent often moves into *chika-ma* range, then you can also use it as a chance to try and practise *debana-waza*.

7. Ji-geiko for a Female Practitioner Facing a Male Opponent

There is a general conception that women have difficulty, or are apprehensive to engage in *ji-geiko* against strong male opponents. However, every practitioner, both male and female, has weak points which can be exploited. There may be a distance that they find awkward to fence from, or there may be a style of kendo that they find different to compete against. This is something that everyone, not just females, should keep in mind.

To overcome weaknesses in ourselves, we must regularly practise *ji-geiko* with those opponents we have difficulty against, as avoiding them is not a solution and our weak points will remain. Remember who these people are, and force yourself to train with them more than with other partners. Conduct your own research and endeavour to find solutions to overcome your weak points.

If, as a female practitioner, you find strong males to be difficult opponents, then you should train with strong males regularly so as not to be at a physical and psychological disadvantage. Generally, if you face a taller opponent they will feel crowded if you move into *chika-ma* range, and this pressure may cause them to make mistakes. They will often find it more difficult to kick off with their left foot from this range. If you wish to employ this strategy, then you must discover how to close in to this range in a manner that is advantageous to yourself. If you simply step in, your opponent will most likely react with a *debana-waza* counterattack, so you must devise ways of closing the distance with various timings and from different angles.

If you meet an opponent's attack square-on with your own *taiatari*, you may be knocked over if there is a significant difference in body weight and power. If this is the case, then *ashi-sabaki* and *tai-sabaki* should be brought into play to compensate.

One final piece of advice for female practitioners is that they should avoid *ji-geiko* with males who have a reputation for bullying those weaker than themselves, or who appear to disregard the benefits of practising with females. There is no benefit for you in training with such people, and there is nothing worthwhile they can teach you. I recommend that you keep away from them, and politely refuse direct invitations to train with them.

8. Summary

When you perform *ji-geiko* with someone, it should be an experience that you want to repeat, not one which makes you scared or reluctant to practise with the same person again. I hope this advice will improve your kendo outlook and enhance your training experiences.

CHAPTER 9

APPROACHES IN SHIAI

1. Introduction

The previous two chapters dealt with *ji-geiko* methodology and attitudes. In this and the next chapter, I will examine the *shiai* component of kendo from various angles. A practitioner's understanding of *shiai* dictates whether their kendo approach is competitive and sport-like in nature, or whether they view kendo as a form of *budō*. These attitudes are apparent in how a practitioner competes, watches other people compete, and how they support others in matches. A better understanding of the nature of *shiai* and kendo's *budō* essence will enrich your kendo experience and improve your relationships with other practitioners. This chapter will examine the purpose of *shiai* and the attitudes of competitors, teams, spectators and instructors towards *shiai*.

2. The Purpose of Shiai in Kendo

The Chinese characters for the word *shiai* literally mean "to test each other", and what this inherently means in kendo is that we test the attitudes, manners, spirit, and skills we have learned in *keiko* by pitting ourselves against an opponent in a competitive situation. Inoue (1994, p. 162) explains: "The purpose of training in modern kendo is to refine one's spirit, which is normally hidden away, and allow spiritual expression through performing physically 'visible' techniques. The practice of *shiai* in kendo must be in line with this purpose." With these words in mind, practitioners of kendo should recognise the important opportunity *shiai* presents us for developing our skills and personality, and endeavour to foster a correct attitude towards personal development.

High school students in Japan whose primary concern is winning in kendo *shiai* are quite often criticised for their bad attitude. During my time at high school I was a prime example of this, although it is somewhat embarrassing to reflect upon it now. I performed rough kendo, and did not worry about what others thought about my technique or form; I only cared about winning. The desire to win is not necessarily a bad thing in itself though; to be fair to yourself and to your opponent, you should always do your best to win. Aiming to develop the skills to win while at the same time nurturing an understanding of the essence of kendo and one's own personality greatly influences how we compete and perform in *shiai*. However, if we consider kendo to be a *budō* rather than simply a competitive sport, then there are certain forms of etiquette and manners we should uphold even when we are trying to win.

3. The Attitudes of Competitors in Shiai

In this section I will not discuss how to fight in a *shiai* because as the opponent and the situation changes, so do the strategies you must apply. Once a *shiai* begins, all decisions about how to compete should be spontaneously made by the individual competitor. It was often the case in Japan that high school kendo coaches would constantly throw instructions and advice at their students during a *shiai*. This belittles the students' autonomy, and hinders the smooth running of matches and the *taikai* in general. We do not see this at official *taikai* anymore, but it still occurs in practice matches.

Regardless of what is happening during the *shiai*, the most important thing is to control yourself. You will never be able to subdue your opponent successfully in a match if you are not in control of your own emotions. You need to be able to minimise nervousness and excitement before and during a *shiai*, and you need to be able to focus on your opponent without any distractions. Do not get too caught up in the moment, but evaluate each of your performances immediately afterwards and be sure to thank your opponents. This process helps you maximise the *shiai* experience and what you can take away from it.

Before a *shiai*, it is important to visualise yourself at optimal performance to bolster your self-confidence. A strong desire to win is important but can lead to impatience, and your opponent may provoke you into making hasty attacks; haste will only end in disaster. You will achieve a calmer and more productive state of mind if your goal is to win by doing your best kendo rather than trying to win at any cost.

From a strategic standpoint it is also important to know who you will fight against, and what their kendo is like. Some people insist that just doing one's own kendo is important and that you should not change your kendo style to suit your opponent. This philosophy also has its merits, but I believe it to be more applicable to beginners who have a small repertoire of techniques and a limited supply of tactics. For others, I would still recommend heightening concentration levels, performance visualisation incorporating how you will fight against the opponent's type of kendo, and devising tactics.

Of course, thinking or strategising too much before a match may lead to confusion and be counter-productive, but good mental preparation will have a marked effect on your *shiai* performance. During *shiai* you are often forced to modify your tactics and to control your emotional stress. These types of decisions and actions must be performed at an instant and is not something you can acquire purely through *ji-geiko*; you must take part in *shiai* and gain experience under pressure.

Competitors should focus only on themselves and their opponents in order to make the best decisions and perform to the best of their ability. Habits such as looking at the *shinpan* to see if a point was scored should be avoided. Even if you think that you have made a perfect strike you should only concentrate on your opponent until you clearly hear an announcement from the *shinpan*.

In an evenly-matched *shiai* you and your opponent will tussle for control, but you may see few opportunities to score. In these kinds of situations, one competitor may lose by making a small tactical error, or by losing concentration momentarily. It is necessary to concentrate fully for the duration of the entire match, and to be able to make appropriate decisions under pressure. Experience in actual *shiai* is the best way to acquire these skills.

Your match performances will also improve if you get into the habit of reflecting on how you fought after each *shiai*. Naturally, there are occasions when you have very little time to get ready for your next match, but I still recommend that you make a quick and simple critique of your match. Often you may not remember exactly what happened if you were nervous or over-excited, or your match was drawn out over a long time. Even so, you might be able to ask people who were watching for their comments, or watch video footage that someone recorded.

There will always be winners and losers in *shiai*, but we need to aim to be humble in victory and gracious in defeat. As I have written elsewhere (Honda, 2003, p. 141), a good winner in kendo is someone who competes fairly and squarely (*seisei-dōdō*), displays modesty, and understands the role of *shiai* in self-development. Even if you win, you must respect the loser's feelings by not showing off. A good loser will display the same attitude and respect as a good winner. On the other hand, a bad winner will make obvious displays of celebration in front of the loser, and a bad loser will display their frustration at losing and not congratulate the winner. Both of these types of people do not understand the essence of *shiai*. We are afforded the opportunity to compete in *shiai* thanks to the cooperation and effort of the other competitors, *shinpan,* recorders, timekeepers and assistants. We should not lose track of the purpose of *shiai*, and should always show gratitude to these people.

4. The Attitudes of Competing Teams and Spectators

During a *taikai* we are not supposed to loudly support or give advice to competitors; on-looking teammates and members of the audience should restrict their support to clapping. This is out of consideration for the competitors and the *shinpan* who need to focus on the action of the *shiai*. Other forms of support or cheering might prove distracting or impede the running of the *taikai*. As mentioned previously I believe strongly that advice should not be given to competitors mid-match, and all decisions and strategies should be left to them to decide.

Competitors should ideally learn to cope with the stress and pressure of *shiai* for themselves without the psychological support or extra pressure from their teammates or spectators. The most distracting element for *shinpan* are camera flashes as they might miss a critical moment of the action when dazzled by a photographer's camera flash. Only with mutual cooperation from all those involved can *taikai* be run fairly, efficiently and enjoyably.

During team matches it was originally standard etiquette for managers, coaches, and team members to sit and watch in *seiza*. It would be awkward, however, if you were to get pins-and-needles in your feet or your legs went numb while waiting for your turn. Nowadays however, managers, coaches, and team members need only sit in *seiza* during the *senpō*, *taishō* matches and any representative matches (*daihyōsha-sen*) that occur. Team members waiting for their turn may stand up one bout before theirs.

Although I previously stated that competitors should learn to cope with stressful *shiai* situations for themselves, it is still important to be involved with your teammates' bouts. Teamwork and camaraderie will bolster a competitor's courage and confidence, and an individual victory is everyone's victory in a team situation.

5. Instructors' Attitudes to Shiai

It is the responsibility of instructors to support their students and encourage them to fight fairly. Proper etiquette and *shiai* demeanour is learned by the instructor's example and attitude in the *dōjō*. Giving feedback to students can be a delicate issue; the self-esteem, ability and motivation level of each individual plays a part in how they take advice from others. Aoki (1996) recommends that, in regular practice in the *dōjō*, performance feedback is most effective when given straight after each match. In the case of *shiai* however, the timing of the feedback may need to be carefully chosen taking into account the individual's and team's result. In certain cases advice may be better left for a later occasion.

6. Summary

The vast majority of kendo practitioners are most likely aware that *shiai* is not the be-all and end-all of kendo; it is just one part of the whole and *shiai* results do not determine the worth of a practitioner. The whole *shiai* process and training cycle are more crucial. In other words, how the individual prepares for, competes in and deals with the *shiai* situation, how they reflect on their performance, and whether they can learn something from the experience and incorporate it into their future training. This kind of pattern will bring out the best in an individual's performances.

If a practitioner has the correct attitude, he or she stands to benefit a great deal from the *shiai* experience. On the other hand, thinking too much about how one should act can often detract from the enjoyment; ideally *shiai* should be fun and exciting as well. We feel elated when we score a perfectly timed *ippon* under *shiai* pressure, and this feeling may motivate us to train harder in the future. A *taikai* is a fascinating event where every competitor can learn important lessons to improve their kendo.

In the next chapter I will introduce some methods of *shiai* practice to be used in regular training. I will also discuss the purpose of squad training sessions.

CHAPTER 10

TRAINING FOR SHIAI

1. Introduction

The previous chapter dealt with the attitudes of competitors, teams, spectators and instructors in *shiai* I pointed out that a practitioner's understanding of *shiai* dictates whether their kendo approach is competitive and sport-like in nature, or whether they view kendo as a form of *budō*. An appreciation of the purposes and benefits of *shiai* will make the experience more enjoyable and memorable, and allow you to have better relations with other practitioners. This chapter covers how to run *shiai* practice matches in your regular training venue. I will investigate the purposes of *shiai* practice, and discuss squad training methodology. I will also outline how I coached the Great Britain Kendo Team to prepare for the 12th World Kendo Championships and other international *taikai*.

This chapter features three kinds of *shiai* practice to be held in your regular club training sessions. The first is the standard *shiai* based on the official rules and regulations. The remaining two are *shiai* styles that have been modified in certain ways to achieve particular training goals.

2. Shiai for Beginners

It is important for seniors in a *dōjō* to organise *shiai* practice regularly so that beginners can experience competing and learn the necessary rules and etiquette. This is also an opportunity for seniors to monitor the progress of juniors and decide what areas of their kendo need improvement. It can be quite time-consuming to have everyone in the *dōjō* fight in turn using only one *shiai-jō*; participants will spend most of their time watching rather than competing. The *shiai* format you choose for practice will most likely depend on the number of members in your *dōjō* and how many of those are able to referee.

If possible, it may be better to divide up into a number of groups and have one person act as *shinpan* on each mini *shiai-jō*. This should put less pressure on juniors, and the number of possible rotations should increase. Under the pressure of the situation, those with little *shiai* experience may find themselves preoccupied with attacking and defending at the expense of certain rules or forms of etiquette. Informal *shiai* practice sessions like this provide the opportunity for seniors to promptly correct the mistakes of juniors and provide technical and tactical advice when necessary.

As juniors progress they can gradually be made aware of *jōgai-hansoku* (stepping out of bounds) and "*Wakare!*" (break), and taking positional advantage in the *shiai-jō*. Also, having juniors fight matches while everyone is watching will add an extra element of pressure when they are ready for it. After getting used to this type of *shiai* practice, those members who are not absolute beginners may be given the chance to experience refereeing while *dōjō* seniors supervise. Rather than learning the technical skills required to be a *shinpan*, these opportunities will enable them to give more consideration to what constitutes a valid *ippon*, and what are the most opportune times to attack.

3. Shiai with a Handicap

When there is a significant difference in levels between juniors and seniors, the rules can be modified by giving more experienced players a handicap and less experienced players an advantage. This not only extends the match time in *shiai* that would otherwise be over very quickly, but allows seniors to have the club's members focus on certain points for improvement.

For example, an experienced member might be instructed to only use *tobikomi-men* or *debana-men* and this would mean that less experienced members can step up to this senior with more confidence than they would normally have. Naturally, the less experienced member would be instructed to use their entire repertoire of techniques (minus *ōji-waza*) without hesitation and would be afforded the opportunity to improve their *ashi-sabaki*, *tai-sabaki* and *shinai* control. As they realise this senior can only attack *men*, they should not be so intimidated or confused during the match. There are also benefits for seniors in these kinds of *shiai* as the more experienced members who receive the handicaps are forced into making more effort to create opportunities to land their *tobikomi-men* or *debana-men* attacks.

In principle, beginners tend to be very defensive as they do not want to be hit, and their cuts tend to be large as they have not been taught how to make proper small strikes yet. In the case where an experienced member and a less experienced member try to strike *men* on each other at the same time, the experienced member's small cut will end up hitting the less experienced member's *shinai* or hands, even if the experienced member's attack is faster. Through this style of *shiai*, more experienced members will be able to improve their timing and distancing skills, and learn how to better lure or pressure their opponent into making the first attack.

4. Shiai Variations

Here is another type of handicapped *shiai* format that allows the practice of specific skills. The members of the *dōjō* who will compete are divided into two teams; one team will play an attack-only role and the other team a defence-only role. *Shiai* time is set from thirty seconds up to one minute. The attack-only team aggressively attempts to strike *ippon* against their opponents without worrying about being hit by *ōji-waza*; if they score, then they win the bout. The defence-only team must use *ashi-sabaki*, *tai-sabaki* and *shinai* control to avoid their opponent's attacks but not attack themselves; if they successfully prevent their opponent from scoring, then they win the bout. This style of practice is useful for developing skills in *renzoku-waza*, *taiatari*, feints, surprise attacks, and defensive manoeuvres.

In the case that the defence-only team are more experienced than their opponents, the area is which they are allowed to move may be restricted. In the case that the attack-only team is more experienced, the targets which they are allowed to attack may be restricted. The attack-only team should not get flustered in their attempts to score or begin swinging the *shinai* around madly trying to outwit their opponents. The *dōjō* seniors must point out and correct any attack or defence manoeuvres that stray too far away from orthodox kendo.

5. Shiai Practice at Squad Training

Squad training generally involves regular repetitions of modified matches, team matches, and squad league matches, and this kind of *shiai* practice is important for coaches to select which members will take part in various regional, national or international *taikai*. The other objectives of squad training include technical and tactical improvement, developing teamwork, and strengthening fighting spirit. The following are three types of *shiai* practice that can be used in squad training sessions.

i) Shiai of three-to-five minutes duration

In this kind of *shiai*, competitors continue fighting until time runs out regardless of how many times they score or are scored against. The aim is to compete continuously for 3-5 minutes but this can be modified according to the number of squad members and visitors, their ability levels, their physical condition, and particular training or *taikai* goals. The objective of this format is to allow squad members the chance to fight to their heart's content, and let them physically remember what a 3-5 minute *shiai* feels like in terms of time and energy. The non-stop scenario means that they will have to concentrate for the entire bout, and keep fighting continuously right until the end.

In a real *shiai* a competitor may land a strike that they feel is valid but the *shinpan* do not acknowledge it. Also, we sometimes encounter an opponent who performs strange, violent or annoying kendo. In other words, we need to be psychologically ready for whatever occurs in a *shiai* as we never know what we may come up against. Whatever happens, becoming upset or annoyed by *shinpan* judgements or by your opponent's kendo will only have a negative effect on your own performance. I stress time and again that you must first learn to control yourself if you hope to be able to control your opponent. The non-stop nature of this kind of *shiai* practice will teach participants to be less frustrated with these irritations.

ii) Shiai under simulated conditions

One example of a simulated scenario would be to award *ippon* to one competitor before the bout starts and reduce *shiai* time to 60-90 seconds to simulate the remaining time in a match in which one competitor has taken the first point already. This kind of practice develops selective technical and tactical ability while simultaneously teaching squad members to fight aggressively without losing their cool or being affected by the time constraint. As mentioned in the previous chapter, I believe that all decisions should be left to competitors once a match has begun. Therefore I do not tell squad members what to do even during this type of *shiai* practice, but I will reprimand them if they become overly obsessed with winning or their kendo is excessively rough. *Shiai* time is short in this type of practice, and so squad members are required to fight again after comparatively short rests. It is important for squad members to maintain a positive attitude and give every match their best even if they perform badly from time to time. If a team manages to keep winning, the intervals between their matches become shorter, so it is good practice for maintaining high spirits in a competitive situation.

iii) Team shiai

This practice format is made as close to real *shiai* as possible by following official rules, using a *shiai-jō* set to official size standards, and using three *shinpan*. The objectives are to simulate the experience of competing in a real *taikai*, to build team spirit, and to learn how each member should compete and support others in their respective positions. This is why it is referred to as "team *shiai*". As a member of a team, there is more to be accomplished than simply winning your own matches. The impression you give the opposition and the effort you make influences your own teammates and can affect how they perform. If we were to use a relay-race metaphor, your mood, attitude, and level of motivation in a team *shiai* can affect the way in which you 'pass the baton' on to the next person to compete. Regardless of your match result, if you have not given it your best shot, your teammates will be well aware, because they have spent so much time training with you and know what kind of kendo you can perform. If you do not make a full effort or have regrets about how you should have performed then this can prove very discouraging for your teammates. Always performing your best kendo is difficult, but the effort you put in is obvious to your teammates and, if you give it your best shot, this will motivate your teammates to perform well too. The baton that you metaphorically pass on to your teammate in team *shiai* is comprised of your effort and fighting spirit, not your win or loss. It is the responsibility of each team member to support their teammates, to do their best, and to not be psychologically affected by the results of each match.

In my position as Great Britain's kendo squad coach in preparation for the 12th World Kendo Championships, I placed emphasis on each member doing their best in their position, and passing on the baton with good fighting spirit, teamwork, and mutual support. I am pleased to say that the men's and women's teams both made great improvements and fought superbly in the championship with a great sense of teamwork and spirit of camaraderie.

6. Summary

This and the previous chapter dealt with various aspects of *shiai*. The fundamental point to always keep in mind is that *shiai* is only one part of what kendo has to offer; it should not be the main goal for practising kendo. Nonetheless, *shiai* plays an important role in personal development and is one vital component that contributes to our growth in kendo. My hope is that kendo practitioners will not view *shiai* in a negative light, or harbour misguided ideas and attitudes about the purposes and nature of *shiai*.

CHAPTER 11

KENDO TACTICS

1. Introduction

This chapter does not describe how to win by pushing the boundaries of regulations in kendo. The word 'tactics' holds many connotations including negative ones such as 'deceitfulness', 'slyness', 'tricking one's opponent or the referees', or 'strategies for winning at any cost'. As such, kendo tactics are often frowned upon, with many instructors refraining from teaching them. On the flip side however, a great deal can be learned about the technical aspects of kendo through the consideration, practice and creation of tactics.

2. Tactics in Kendo

Alongside elements such as physical fitness, technique and mental strength, tactics play an important role in the performance of sports and *budō* alike. In kendo circles however, negative undertones often surround the notion of tactics. This usually stems from the instructor's ideology on whether kendo is a martial art (*budō*) or simply a competitive sport.

In a survey targeting physical education teachers in charge of kendo training in Japanese high schools (Honda, 2003), 53 out of the 55 respondents indicated negativity regarding the teaching of tactics. They responded, as they consider kendo to be a *budō* rather than a sport, that the traditional training, teachings, postures and movements, as well as the win-lose scenario of competitions are all an important part of character development. Many of them stated that kendo is only being practised 'correctly' if the goal of training is character development or self-improvement. They view tactical kendo being taught for the sole purpose of winning in competition as a deviation from kendo's true path.

Traditionally, the initial training period in a martial art was called *shugyō* and involved countless repetitions of *kihon*. Some teachers believe that correct posture and *shinai* control must be learned in this way and tactics rejected because they may lead practitioners away from what is considered 'correct kendo'. In other words, they believe that employing strategies or modifying techniques so that an individual or team can win generally results in a sacrifice of correct form.

If kendo is to be viewed as a *budō* and not as a sport then opponents should face off against each other using their *ki*. In doing so, practitioners can gauge their progress and identify their weaknesses. For many practitioners, overwhelming an opponent with one's *ki* is what represents true kendo and so one's mental state is of utmost importance. If for the sake of tactics, too much emphasis is placed on technical cleverness, then wasteful *shinai* and body movement may result which strays from *budō* ideals.

Non-Japanese people, especially those who play Western sports, may think that these views are somewhat strange from a sporting point of view, however kendo is a one-on-one 'combative activity' involving attacks and defensive manoeuvres using a bamboo sword. Kern (1998) observes that one-on-one combative activities require greater tactical acumen in performance than non-physical contact activities such as volleyball and tennis, activities that a certain number of athletes play in a game or race at the same time such as swimming and boat racing, and activities which are not played simultaneously, where performance is compared by time, distance, height and judges' scoring such as gymnastics and weight lifting. In fact all kendo exponents, both in *ji-geiko* and *shiai*, make use of tactics both consciously and unconsciously during attack and defence.

Many of the kendo teachers who participated in the aforementioned survey also pointed out that kendo skills ideally should not be drawn from one's physical strength, but should come from one's *ki* power and striking motion. Despite the high level of this ideal, it is still a form of tactic. Even taking this one step further to the highest level of kendo where the individual operates in a state of "no-mind" (*mushin*) is still a tactical approach acquired through much experience and a high level of technical prowess.

Nonetheless, it appears that the notion of 'tactics' does not sit well with many Japanese kendo teachers as they feel that employing tactics means that their students might start to see winning as their sole motivation and strive for victory at any cost. Whatever the instructor's reasons for rejecting the teaching of tactics, and whatever their ideologies of kendo as *budō* are, I believe that these all come from their love of kendo and the idea that they want to pass on "correct kendo" to the next generation as a pathway for self-cultivation and as a part of traditional Japanese culture.

3. My Experiences at Fukuoka University of Education

Although I competed in many *shiai* and practice-*shiai* while a student at high school and university, my kendo teachers hardly ever showed me how to fight or win in particular situations. Was this due to the fact that the notion of 'tactics' often held a negative connotation in Japanese kendo circles? Development of tactics was largely left to each individual, and so I acquired tactics naturally through my own experiences and by watching other people.

I began giving more serious consideration to tactics when I became the coach for the women's kendo club at Fukuoka University of Education. The club's members were aiming to win the All Japan University Women's Championship and so were practising in two-hour sessions five times a week; something not unusual for university kendo clubs in Japan. In addition, a training method that I introduced was to gather in my office and watch the videos I had taped of their *keiko* and *shiai*, and discuss how improvements could be made. I initially made the suggestion to record their performances, but the team members themselves decided what aspects they would pay attention to and how they would improve individually and as a team.

After continuing this self-evaluation for seven months, the team began to grasp what each member was expected to do in their respective positions, how to fight, and how they should adapt according to different competition circumstances. They achieved their goal in November 1995 and did not have to resort to tactics such as keeping an unnecessary distance from stronger opponents, avoiding further contact after the taking the first point, or using surprising or tricky attacks at the expense of good posture.

Their success was due to their constant reflection on *keiko* and *shiai* performances, discussions on how to handle different types of opponents in various situations, trial of new approaches, and development of the scope of their kendo. Three years later, two of them were selected as members of the Japanese team for the 11th World Kendo Championships, and one went on to win the women's individual division.

Through the experience of being their coach, my thoughts about tactics began to change. In the majority of kendo lessons, very little is taught about tactics. Although a few books and some research on the topic of tactics in kendo exist, in my opinion the descriptions are too abstract to effectively understand and apply in practice. For that reason I went to the United Kingdom in 1997 and enrolled in a doctoral program to study the theories, practices and educational effects of sporting tactics. I followed a system called *Teaching Games for Understanding* which had been developed in England, and I attempted to apply it to kendo instruction. Through my study of tactics I realised that they are useful not only for winning *shiai*, but also can also aid in the understanding of various other aspects of kendo.

4. Re-consideration of Tactics in Kendo

Tactics play a role in connecting *kihon-geiko* with *ji-geiko* and *shiai*. We apply techniques that we have acquired in *kihon-geiko* during *ji-geiko* and *shiai* in a tactical way, considering which techniques to use in which situations, and how to use them properly. Most kendo clubs begin practice with a warm-up and *suburi* followed by *kirikaeshi*, *kihon-waza-geiko* and then *ji-geiko*. Tactical training, in which the object would be to teach which technique and when, where and how to use it, is neglected and left to the individual to develop through their own experiences. There is a great flux in attacking and defending in *ji-geiko* and *shiai*, so it is difficult to decide what to do ahead of time; split-second judgements are left to each competitor's discretion.

It is important, however, to learn tactics in *keiko* in order to make an appropriate judgement and execute the chosen action. Some experienced practitioners believe that tactics are not necessary, and that fighting in the state of *mushin* is the best approach to employ in *ji-geiko* and *shiai*. Accordingly, in this supreme mental state, one's mind would subconsciously act and react allowing the most appropriate choice of technique and movement. However, if one does not spend a great deal of time consciously learning and internalising the tactical attack and defence patterns for various situations, the state of *mushin* would prove ineffective.

Some other practitioners insist that "doing one's own kendo" consistently and not modifying one's actions or tactics for different opponents is what is important. I am forced to disagree with this view as it implies that we should only use the same *waza* with the same timing regardless of what kind of opponent we face. Kendo is certainly not static in this way, and performing well against a variety of opponents requires subtle or sometimes radical alterations in *seme, waza* and timing.

To accomplish this one must develop a wide repertoire of *waza* and broaden one's scope in kendo. Merely learning lots of different *waza* will not ensure success; one should practise with consideration to how each *waza* can be used effectively. My teacher Masatake Sumi once told me that he has memorised a great number of different patterns of *seme*, attack and counterattack, and that he can draw on any of these in response to different opponents and situations. At this level he is able to exert great control over less experienced opponents, and lead them into making the attacks he chooses allowing him to counterattack in a pre-planned manner. It is extremely difficult to reach this level, but we should all try.

5. Summary

Once you start to give consideration to tactics in *ji-geiko* and *shiai*, you are obliged to examine both your technical strengths and weaknesses. You will be better able to recognise the technical and psychological structure of basic movements, *waza* and interaction with opponents. Another positive side-effect of this line of inquiry is that you will feel an increased desire to not waste any of your training time and to improve your physical and mental fitness to enable successful execution of newly acquired tactics. The traditional approach in kendo training is repeated practice of basics, and the vast majority of the kendo population, including myself, would not discount the merits of this methodology. By studying tactics you will be able to take responsibility for your own development in *keiko* rather than relying solely on what your teacher tells you.

CHAPTER 12

LOWER TACTICS

1. Introduction

The previous chapter covered the role and effectiveness of tactics in kendo and included some of my own personal study experiences. In this chapter we will discuss the study of tactics as they apply to a practitioner's individual skill level. It should be pointed out again that I am not describing how to win competitions by stretching the limits of kendo rules. My hope is that you will be able to better develop your understanding of the technical aspects of kendo through the process of devising and implementing tactics. This chapter deals with the subject of learning tactics for both holders of *kyū* grades and lower *dan* grades (1st and 2nd).

2. Tactics for Kyū Grades

Kyū grade holders often repeat large *men* attacks from the same distance with the same timing during *ji-geiko*, *shiai* and *shinsa* (examinations). Their teachers encourage this approach with their advice to "Keep attacking!", or "Give it everything you've got!" There is a tendency for other inexperienced competitors to mirror this style of attack which leads to both sides clashing their *shinai* in the middle as they both strike simultaneously and unsuccessfully. This often continues for prolonged periods with no points being scored.

As I have explained previously, it is important for less experienced practitioners to put the techniques they have learned in *kihon-geiko* into action without hesitation or fear. This in itself is a simple yet important tactic, however you will not create many openings to attack your opponent if you repeat a similar attacking sequence from the same distance, with the same timing. In kendo there are four opportunities to strike your opponent:

- When your opponent begins to make their strike
- When your opponent blocks your strike
- When your opponent finishes making their strike
- When your opponent makes a retreating movement backwards

Of these four, the third is an important for holders of *kyū* grades to learn and practise during *ji-geiko* with those of a similar grade. To give a specific example, in *kihon-geiko* holders of *kyū* grades tend to go through on either side of their opponent after attacking, exposing their back completely just like they do in *kihon-geiko*. In shiai, however, this would actually leave them open to attack at the instant they turn around to face their opponent. When your opponent runs by you in *ji-geiko*, practitioners can make a habit of following and attacking them. The merit of practising this tactic is that an individual will learn the importance of always keeping an eye on their opponent, and remember that an opportunity to strike is presented when the opponent looks away.

When *kyū* grade holders have *ji-geiko* with their seniors, they tend to feel, difficulty in completing their attack and stop after only executing half of the cutting movement and then move back in an awkward way. More experienced practitioners will rarely turn away from their opponent, and *kyū* grade holders will experience trouble attempting to strike these kinds of opponents with this kind of timing. When practising *ji-geiko* against seniors, I recommend that holders of *kyū* grades try to overpower their opponent's *shinai* before striking. This means deflecting the tip of your opponent's *shinai* first rather than simply launching a straight-in attack. Techniques include *osae-waza* (holding the opponent's *shinai* down) and *harai-waza* (knocking the opponent's *shinai* off the centreline).

These techniques alone will not guarantee that you score a point. Your attack will probably be blocked, but at this stage it is important to start learning how to break the opponent's control of the centreline. No matter how simple it is, this tactic of breaking the opponent's control of the centreline is further developed into more complex and effective strategies as the individual's footwork, *fumikiri*, *fumikomi*, speed and *tenouchi* improve, but these will be explained in more detail later.

As previously discussed, *kyū* grade holders should focus mainly on developing their *shikake-waza* skills. Therefore it is important that you not be afraid of having your attack evaded or being counterattacked by a more experienced opponent. At this stage you should also complete all of your attacks and not stop midway through a motion because you worry that the attack will not succeed. I suggest that you use *osae-waza* and *harai-waza* in both your *waza-geiko* and *ji-geiko*.

Although not directly related to tactics, I should reiterate something about defence in kendo; it is important to keep in mind the expression "*bōgyo no tame no bōgyo nashi*". In kendo, this means that if a defence is static and does not allow the practitioner to flow into a counterattack afterwards, then it is inefficient. In traditional kendo terminology the superior strategy is referred to as *kōbō-itchi* or the "union of attack and defence".

The next problem for a *kyū* grade holder is that they lack the skills and reflexes to successfully counterattack a senior practitioner by using *ōji-waza*. This is also often linked to the fact that they may have not initially acquired the basic skills to defend against an opponent's attack. As I have already covered, strangely enough, methods of defence are seldom taught but are left to practitioners to learn for themselves through experience or by copying others.

Because of this, many *kyū* grade holders try to defend in their own ways when they are attacked by their seniors, and they have no opportunity to learn the idea of "*bōgyo no tame no bōgyo nashi*". Okajima (1992) points out that a beginner's anxiety and fear of their opponent's attacking would prevent them from finding opportunities for a strike. It is suggested again, therefore, that teachers impart basic defence techniques to beginners before they are allowed to join *ji-geiko*. What I mean by basic defence techniques is not to defend by merely using one's *shinai* to block with. What one has to learn is *metsuke* (positioning of the eyes) and defence with *ki-ken-tai-no-itchi*. Beginners tend to stand and gaze only at their opponent's *shinai*, and their hands tend to move as the opponent moves his/her *shinai*. Therefore, they are quite often easily caught by feints such as pretending to attack *men* by lifting the arms up and actually attacking *dō*.

According to the *Japanese-English Dictionary of Kendo* (p. 62), *metsuke* is explained as "the act of paying attention to the opponent's whole body while looking into his/her eyes." In addition, there is also another term to teach us how to look at the opponent called *enzan-no-metsuke* as introduced in Chapter 6. The *Japanese-English Dictionary of Kendo* (2000, p. 24) explains, "it is important to look at the figure of the opponent as a whole rather than at a particular points, as if looking at a far away mountain."

As for defence with *ki-ken-tai-no-itchi*, when one defends, one needs to keep a positive mind and use effective *shinai* handling, footwork and body movement. The term *ki-ken-tai-no-itchi* is normally used for expressing the striking action, but this idea should also be applied to defence. It is not easy for beginners to do this. However, it is in your best interests to develop your kendo through being struck over and over again, keeping proper posture and effective defensive positioning, which will not necessarily be effective at first. In the future, you will develop the skill to defend in the most effective way. Okajima (1992) argues that strong defence is an important element in performance in kendo. If that is so, then learning defensive techniques with an understanding of *bōgyo no tame no bōgyo nashi* at this stage will be quite useful towards helping to execute high level tactics in the future.

3. Tactics for 1-*dan* and 2-*dan*

It is assumed that practitioners at this level can make sharp strikes with small and quick hand movements and powerful *fumikiri* and *fumikomi*. I suggest therefore that they develop simple tactics based on *osae-waza* and *harai-waza* and attack after leading with a feint. Practitioners should know that even if they try to strike *men* after using *osae-waza*, an experienced opponent will still have time to react and block the attack unless it is very fast. The same result may occur when they try to strike *kote* after using *harai-waza* to knock their opponent's *shinai* to the side; their opponent generally senses what is going to happen and is able to react to avoid the *kote* strike. In these situations an effective tactic is to use a feinting action before striking. Here are two simple examples:

1. Hold your opponent's *shinai* down with an *osae-waza* and then pretend to attack their *men*. When your opponent moves to protect themselves against the impending *men* attack, then you can attack their open *kote* or *dō* instead.
2. Knock your opponent's *shinai* aside from left to right and then pretend to attack the exposed *kote* target. When your opponent moves to protect against the impending *kote* attack, then you can attack their open *men* instead.

The following is a more complex example:

3. Knock your opponent's *shinai* aside from left to right and then pretend to attack *kote-men*. After you first launch into the *kote* attack the opponent will then move to cover their *men*, then you can attack their open *dō*.

When using these feinting actions you must remember that it is important to take the initiative, outwit your opponent and seize the presented opportunity to strike. It is also important that this process should be done in one smooth flowing motion. The opponent will read your intention and your attack will fail if you wait for the target to be open before starting your striking motion. At first I recommend starting by having a clear idea of the pattern of the entire technique. This means that you will have a predetermined idea of the opponent's reaction to your *seme* and the chance that it will create. The final part of the pattern is to make an accurate strike and finish properly with the appropriate *kime* and *zanshin*. After you understand the entire pattern of the technique it is time to try to put it into practice in *ji-geiko*.

Through this process you will examine what distance, timing, footwork and *shinai* handling are appropriate for different feinting and striking actions. By repeating mistakes, you will gradually increase and refine your pattern of attacking. This process of trial and error will also make you realise what techniques you need to improve.

It is also assumed that practitioners at this level have some kind of *tokui-waza*, a speciality technique that they can perform well and often score with. In addition to feint tactics, I recommended practitioners investigate when and how they can most effectively employ their *tokui-waza*. In doing so, consider the following points:

- How long after the start of a *ji-geiko* or *shiai* match do you attempt your *tokui-waza*?
- What are the best conditions for attempting your *tokui-waza*? e.g. distance, timing
- What kind of opponent is your *tokui-waza* effective/ineffective against?

Are you able to visualise particular situations and various kinds of opponents? If you can bring these things to mind, it is an indication that you know your own style of kendo well. Even if you do not think that you have a *tokui-waza*, there must be a favourite technique that you can start thinking of tactics for effective use in *ji-geiko* and *shiai*. Either way, I suggest you reflect on your performance after each *ji-geiko* session. As previously mentioned, these processes will help you develop your tactical abilities while simultaneously deepening your understanding of the technical and psychological structure of kendo, and the mechanical interactions of each *waza*.

Another line of tactics is found in *sute-waza* (throw-away techniques) or *mise-waza* (set-up techniques). In the case of *sute-waza*, you are not concerned whether the technique results in a point as it is sacrificed for another purpose. In the case of *mise-waza*, you perform the same technique a few times to illicit a predictable reaction and set-up an opportunity to suddenly use a different attack to score. Both *sute-waza* and *mise-waza* can be used to create an opportunity to strike with your *tokui-waza*. The following are two simple examples:

- **To perform a *katsugi-men* technique to score a point:**
  Repeatedly attack your opponent's *kote* with a sharp and powerful motion. When you move in again and your opponent alters their *kamae* or moves the *shinai* to cover *kote*, their *men* is then left open for you to strike with *katsugi-men*.

- **To perform a *kote-dō* combination to score a point:**
  Attack your opponent with *kote-men* a few times until they come to expect a *kote-men* combination. Following each *kote* attack, they will most likely raise their arms to block an impending *men* attack; the result being their *dō* is left open for you to strike.

Regardless of whether you are using *sute-waza* or *mise-waza*, the attacking motion should be made not just with your hands but with your whole body. Otherwise your strategy will not be convincing and your opponent may not react in the desired manner, or you may receive an unexpected counterattack.

4. Summary

By gaining further experience in this manner, you are expected not only to develop your *tokui-waza* and other favourite techniques, but also improve *waza* that you are not good at and become able to deal with the kinds of opponents that you generally have difficulty with. If you avoid practising *ji-geiko* with the kinds of opponents that you find difficult, then the situation will never be solved and they will remain your constant weak-point. To rectify the problem, you should try to practise *ji-geiko* with them more than anyone else. Although you might continually lose to them, you will never overcome the problem by overlooking it.

Development in kendo is about learning through hard knocks, not by avoiding them. Trying out new techniques and strategies is also important, but do not try too many new things at once; set tasks for each session and work on short-term goals one at a time. In setting these tasks and goals you should always take into account a realistic appraisal of your abilities, and factor in your instructor's teachings and personal advice. The final chapter of this book will deal with the tactics for holders of the 3-*dan* and above.

CHAPTER 13

HIGHER TACTICS

1. Introduction

The previous chapter dealt with the study of tactics from *kyū* up to 2-*dan* grade holders. In this chapter I will introduce tactics for 3-*dan* to 5-*dan* practitioners, beginning with *keiko* methodology and the development of tactics for various types of opponents. This will be followed by in-depth discussion of kendo's so-called "four opportunities to strike". Previous discussions involved examples of striking when your opponent finishes making their strike, and when your opponent blocks your first strike. This chapter deals with the remaining two opportunities: striking when your opponent begins to make a strike, and when your opponent retreats backwards. Particular attention will be paid to luring your opponent into attacking or retreating through the use of your right leg and *seme* pressure.

2. Tactics for 3-*dan* to 5-*dan*

When you develop tactics for *ji-geiko* at this level, it is important to consider the types of opponents you will face, and the styles of kendo they use. For example, types of opponents may include those who are tall or short, those whose *kensen* is high or low, or slightly to the right, those whose stance is long, short or wide, those whose back foot is angled diagonally left, those whose weight is more on their right leg or left, those whose posture is straight, those who are learning forward or backward, and so on. The types of kendo these opponents use may include those who hold their *shinai* tightly or softly, those who do not use *tenouchi* and simply rely on power, those who are fast, those who are proficient at or tend to favour *debana-waza*, *kaeshi-waza*, *hiki-waza* or *renzoku-waza*, those who use feint techniques, and so on.

Many teachers propound the importance of performing "one's own kendo" no matter what opponent you face, or what situation you find yourself in. However, it can be argued that if you apply the same strategies against all types of opponents, it is unlikely that you will perform well in a competitive sense. Hence, it is important to analyse various types of opponents and styles of kendo so that you can handle them all successfully.

Consider the following questions in relation to your own *dōjō* or club:

• What types of opponents and what types of kendo do you encounter regularly?
• What footwork, *shinai* control, body movements, *waza* and combinations are you using against them?

In the previous discussion of *tokui-waza*, I commented that visualisation is important, and that how well you can perform it is an indication of how well you know your own kendo. Here, once again, visualisation is necessary in analysing types of opponents and styles of kendo. Performing "one's own kendo" does not mean you have to attack with the same timing and the same *waza* all the time regardless of your opponent. Your fighting methods and tactics should change according to your opponent, their style of kendo, and the circumstances you are under.

This does not mean employing strategies that you are not familiar with, or attacks that you have not practised much before. You need to be able to consciously or unconsciously choose the best course of action from an array of options. An individual with a narrow range of strategy or a small repertoire of techniques will not have many choices to rely on, and the kind of kendo they perform will naturally be limited. Such a practitioner may perform well against a certain type of opponent or style of kendo, but may be no match for others. From a coaching perspective, I would hesitate in choosing this kind of individual as a member of a team for competition.

So what tactics can we employ to be able to adapt to various types of opponents and their respective fighting styles? As is it impossible to list every possible strategy, let us begin with suggestions for how practitioners can develop and refine their own.

I previously stressed the importance of having regular *ji-geiko* sessions with those you have difficulty winning against. These types of opponents are an excellent starting point for developing your own strategies. To take this one step further would be to experiment by actually mimicking the types of kendo of these opponents and trying them out for yourself. Most of us have copied the kendo of someone we admire at some point; using their *kamae*, footwork, posture and attacking style. This is a valuable experience and trying to copy the kendo of someone you have difficulty winning against can be beneficial as well.

You may be almost able to imagine that you are that person and try out their kendo in some *ji-*

geiko sessions. I am certain that you will come to identify some of the strengths and weaknesses of that person's *seme*. If you mimic the person's style when practising against a junior, you should be able to immediately see its strengths; and if you use the same style against a senior they should be able to help you identify its weaknesses.

3. Force your Opponent to Strike or Retreat

Of kendo's "four opportunities to strike", I advised that striking your opponent as they finish making a strike is an important tactic for *kyū* grade holders during *ji-geiko* with others of similar grade. For the benefit of *shodan* and 2-*dan* practitioners, I also described using feinting actions and attacking with *sute-waza* and *mise-waza* to set up opportunities to use your *tokui-waza*; a strategy based on striking when your opponent blocks your first strike. Now, in addition to these fundamentals, holders of 3-*dan* and above should focus on the other two opportunities for striking:

- When your opponent begins to make their strike
- When your opponent makes a retreating movement backwards

Practitioners at this level should already employ proper *tenouchi* in the execution of both *shikake-waza* and *ōji-waza*. Consistently using correct *tenouchi* throughout a *ji-geiko* session is difficult, but practitioners at this level must be able to at least employ proper *tenouchi* consistently during *waza-geiko* when there is less pressure on them to perform well, and movements are pre-planned.

In my experience however, there are not many practitioners of this level outside of Japan who consistently demonstrate correct *tenouchi* even during *waza-geiko*. *Tenouchi* is the key to attacking and defending without relying on physical power, and so it allows people to practise together irrespective of differences in age, gender and physique. Ultimately, *tenouchi* is what allows kendo practitioners to continue practising kendo into their old age. As we are discussing tactics I will not deviate by describing methods of performing correct *tenouchi*. Note that the following training strategies are based on the assumption that the practitioner is already competent in using *tenouchi*.

4. Seme in More Detail

It should be obvious to 3-*dan* to 5-*dan* grade holders that, when an opponent has physically begun to strike or to move back, it is generally too late and you have already missed your chance to attack. The strategies outlined here do not entail you waiting for your opponent to take either of these actions so that you may strike; they involve you consciously forcing your opponent into taking these actions when you so desire.

The *Japanese-English Dictionary of Kendo* (2000, p. 83) states that *seme* is to "take the initiative to close the distance with the opponent with full spirit" and that it "puts the opponent off balance mentally and physically and prevents him/her from moving freely". However this definition gives the impression that *seme* can only be employed at a close distance and in one generic manner. It is my opinion that pressure generated by *seme* can be either physical and/or mental and can be employed at any distance and in any situation. Even in *tsubazeriai*, when you cannot physically move any closer to your opponent, you must still apply pressure *seme* psychologically to unsettle your opponent.

Due to this book's length restrictions I will only discuss some *seme* methods from positions of mutual *kamae*. These *seme* methods are the key to learning how to pressure your opponent into attacking or pressuring them into retreating.

5. Seme from Kamae and Use of the Right Leg

It would be impossible to list all of the potential *seme* methods that exist in kendo, so instead this section will cover the use of the right leg in effective *seme*. Traditionally in kendo, the right leg was referred to as the "*seme-ashi* (pressuring/attacking leg)" and the left leg as the "*chikara-ashi* (power leg)". Movement of the right leg must be light and smooth to pressure the opponent into initiating an attack. There must be a dynamic connection of power along the left side of the body (foot, lower leg, knee, thigh, hip and lower back) and, after *fumikiri* is performed, your left leg must always be brought up to complete the proper *hikitsuke* motion.

If however, the distance between your right and left foot makes your stance too long from front to rear, then your centre of gravity will rock backwards and forwards causing your upper-body to lean backwards and forwards during *seme* movements. This lack of solid positioning means that your ability to observe your opponent will become unsettled, and it will be easier for your opponent to discern the timing of your incoming strikes from the large transitions of your centre of gravity and long stance.

To effectively lure your opponent into attacking or retreating, both legs must be used in a coordinated fashion. To alleviate this problem, practitioners must understand the respective roles of their *seme-ashi* and *chikara-ashi* and streamline their *seme* motions to be smaller and more effective.

The first prerequisite is that you be physically and mentally ready to attack or counterattack your opponent from the moment you take your initial *kamae* until the instant you squat down into *sonkyo* afterwards. There is a well-known saying that "kendo begins and ends with *rei*"; however, I do not think that this only applies to kendo's displays of etiquette. From the moment you face your opponent and bow, your fight has already begun and it is important to remain focused on your opponent until the final *rei* .

If you practise *keiko* with this attitude consistently, you will discover the most suitable weight placement for *seme*, the most appropriate length for your stance, the most effective way to control your *kensen*, and the best angle at which to stretch your left leg and bend your right knee. If your attitude to how you take *kamae* changes, your footwork will change, your posture will change, your *seme* will change, and your kendo will change as a whole.

The right leg actually has two roles: the "pressuring/attacking leg" role, and the role of "radar leg" to detect the intentions of your opponent. *Ji-geiko*, *shiai* and *shinsa* normally begin with each practitioner trying to probe the other's defences to discover their intentions, and what style of kendo they use while simultaneously applying pressure with their own tactics. To maximise this pressuring process, slide your right foot slightly forward (without leaning forward) while maintaining a feeling of connectedness in the left side of your body. *Shinai* control also plays an important role in applying pressure and enticing attacks from an opponent through the use of *osae*, *harai* and vertical or straight-in *kensen* movement.

If your opponent does not react to your *seme* attempts, or you feel uncomfortable with your timing, distancing or balance, then you can bring your left foot forward to compensate, and slide your right foot forward again to repeat the process. Alternatively, you may simply withdraw your right foot after its initial forward slide to resume the original distance of the encounter without having moved the left foot at all.

There are additional ways to use the right leg. You could also:

• Stamp on the floor sharply to unsettle your opponent
• Bend your right knee slightly as if bracing for an attack

If you would like to get closer to the opponent (especially a tall one) without your movements being so obvious, then you can bring your left foot up first and slide your right foot forward in a subtle *tsugi-ashi* style. If during the course of this *seme* pressuring an unexpected opportunity to strike is presented, then you should always be ready to respond immediately.

If your opponent retreats backwards under the pressure that you apply then you can do the following:

• Follow them and increase the pressure
• Strike any openings that you detect

Alternatively, if the pressure that you apply elicits an attack from your opponent then you can:

• Take the initiative and strike with *debana-waza*
• Counterattack with *ōji-waza*

What you need to be careful of is the timing as you bring up your left foot. It is quite difficult to react if your opponent attacks when you are only midway through bringing your left forwards. Many experienced practitioners will aim for this moment and take the chance to score *tobikomi-men*.

6. Summary

All of the high-level exponents that I know stand straight and firm, their left leg bracing their movement so they will not be caught out mid-step by their opponent, and to ensure that they can attack at any time. They use their right foot and *shinai* to lure their opponents into making a *men* attack so that they can counterattack with *kaeshi-dō* for example. Alternatively they pressure their opponent to move backwards, and then immediately follow with *men* or *kote-men*.

The tactics outlined in this chapter are just some examples from a wide range of *seme* strategies that are available to the interested practitioner. Practising these kinds of strategies will take your kendo one-notch higher, and allow you to develop the kind of approach to kendo that you can continue into your elderly years.

AFTERWORD

It has been nearly five years since I left the United Kingdom and came back to Japan. I am currently teaching Physical Education at the Fukuoka University of Education. I am also the head instructor of the university kendo club. My ten years in the UK gave me the opportunity to meet many wonderful *kendō-ka*. They are of course not only British, but practitioners from many different countries. The time I spent with them both inside and outside the *dōjō*, and the experiences I had were irreplaceable in my life. I often reflect on what I learned from everyone about what kind of *kendō-ka* and person I should aspire to be.

Even though I am now living in Fukuoka, I still keep in touch with many kendo friends from various countries. Since returning to Japan, I have visited the UK, China, Hong Kong, Italy, Singapore and Russia. I have also had many visitors to my university club from the UK, Canada, China, Chile, France, Hong Kong, Italy, Korea, Malaysia, Mexico and Thailand. Some of them are old friends from my time in the UK, and some are new friends met either in Japan or the countries that I have visited since moving to Fukuoka. I hope that we will continue our friendships and can visit and practise together. I would also very much like to visit new countries that I have not yet been to, and make more new friends through kendo.

As many readers may have already experienced, if there is someone you are hesitant to talk to for the first time, after having *keiko* together you begin to get to know them and find it easier to approach them. In a situation where you have a quarrel with someone, after having *keiko* together you begin to feel like making up, working together and supporting each other again. *Keiko* connects people and also gives us the opportunity to meet new people of all ages. I love kendo as it gives me opportunities to interact with others, and I love people who love kendo.

This book was written based on my ten years of experience and study in the UK, and my sincere desire to help *kendō-ka* who practise hard and teach in sometimes difficult conditions and circumstances which differ from those in Japan.

Half of the chapters in this book were originally articles that I wrote for the *British Kendo Association Newsletter* between 2004 and 2006. The other half were articles for a segment called "Kendo Inside Out" published in *Kendo World* Vol. 3, No. 2, 2005-Vol. 4, No. 2, 2008. During the process of putting all of these articles together and making them into a book, I was given an enormous amount of support from many people.

First, I would like to thank Mr. Ian Parker-Dodd and Mrs. Gillian Parker-Dodd, Mr. Pablo Marchant and Mrs. Yoshimi Marchant for their sincere support and the constant encouragement they gave to my family while we were in the UK. I would also like to thank Mr. Bruce Flanagan and Mr. Max Davies who always helped me by reading my articles and checking my English. I also owe special thanks to Dr. Alex Bennett whose work I have been admiring since I started this project and who gave me the opportunity to write the articles for *Kendo World* and publish this book. I am indebted to Masatake Sumi Hanshi, my *sensei*, who has been always a good and inspiring mentor. My final, and most important thanks must go to three people, Yoko, Haruka and Saki, my wife and daughters. I cannot do kendo without their understanding and support.

"We help each other and develop together in kendo"

Sotaro Honda
March, 2012

REFERENCES

All Japan Kendo Federation, *Fundamental Kendo*, Tokyo: Japan Publication Inc., 1974
————*Kendo Fundamentals Vol. 1, Kendo Equipment, Courtesies, Basic Movements*,
     Tokyo: Satō-Inshokan Inc., 1994
————*Kendo Fundamentals Vol. 2, Personal Attack and Defence Skills, Training (Keiko)*,
     Tokyo: Satō-Inshokan Inc.,1995
————*Japanese-English Dictionary of Kendo*, Tokyo: Satō-Inshokan Inc., 2000
————*Nippon Kendo Kata Instruction Manual*, Tokyo: Satō-Inshokan Inc., 2002

Aoki, T., "Supōtsu to Kokoro - Shinrigaku Shiten" (Psychological Perspectives of Sports and the Mind), Nisugi, S. (ed.), et al, *Supōtsu-gaku no Shiten* (*Sports Studies Perspectives*), pp. 114-128, Kyoto: Shōwadō, 1996

Budden, P. *Looking at a Far Mountain: A Study of Kendo Kata*, London: Ward Lock, 1992

Craig, D. D. *The Heart of Kendo*, London: Shambhala Publication, Inc., 1999

Donohue, J. J. *Herding the Ox: The Martial Arts as Moral Metaphor*, Hartford: Turtle Press, 1998
————*Complete Kendo*, Boston: Tuttle Publishing, 1999

European Kendo Federation, "European Kendo Federation Newsletter", 2001

Honda, S. *Budo or Sport? Competing Conceptions of Kendo within the Japanese Upper Secondary Physical Education Curriculum* (Ph.D. Thesis), University of Gloucestershire - Park Campus Learning Centre, 2003

Inoue, M., *Kendō to Ningen Kyōiku (Kendo and Human Education)*, Tokyo: Tamagawa University Press, 1994

Inoue, Y. *Kendo Kata: Essence and Application* (trans. by Alex Bennett), Auckland: Kendo World Publications, 2003

Kern, J. (trans. Asaoka, Mizukami & Nakagawa), *Supōtsu no Senjutsu Nyūmon* (*Tactics in Sports*), Tokyo: Taishūkan Publishing Co. Ltd., 1998

Kiyota. M. *The Shambhala Guide to Kendo*, Boston: Shambhala Publication, Inc., 1995

Ozawa, H. *Kendo: The Definitive Guide* (trans. by Angela Turzynski). Tokyo: Kodansha International Ltd., 1997

Okajima, H., *Zenkoku Kyōiku-Kei Daigaku Kendō Renmei - Zeminaaru Gendai Kendo - Koseiteki na Waza-zukuri no Sidō-ho* (Instructional Methodology to Encourage the Development of

REFERENCES

Original Techniques - Modern Kendo Seminar - National Kendo Federation for Universities of Education), pp. 140-148, Tokyo: Madosha, 1992

Kosei-teki na Waza-zukuri no Shidō-hō (Teaching Methods for Making Individual Techniques) in *Zenkoku Kyōiku-Kei Daigaku Kendō Renmei* (ed.), *Zeminaaru Gendai Kendō*, pp. 140-148. Tokyo: Madosha Ltd., 1992

Sasamori, J. and Warner, G. *This is Kendo The Art of Japanese Fencing*, Tokyo: Tuttle Publishing, 1964

Sumi, M. *Kendō Nendai-betsu Keiko-hō - Michi-no-Kaori* (Kendo for Every Age: The Scent of the Way), Tokyo: Taiiku to Sports Shuppansha, 2000

Tomiki, K. *Budō-ron* (Budō Theory), Tokyo: Taishukan Publishing Co. Ltd., 1991

GLOSSARY

A
- Ai-men: Simultaneous strike to the head (*men*).
- Asa-geiko: Morning training session.
- Ashi-sabaki: Footwork.
- Ayumi-ashi: A type of footwork akin to normal walking.

B
- Bokutō: Wooden sword.
- Bokutō ni yoru kendō kihon-waza keiko-hō: Training method for kendo fundamentals using a wooden sword.
- Bōgu: Set of kendo armour (*men*, *dō*, *tare*, *kote*).
- Bōgyo no tame no bōgyo nashi: No defence is the best defence.
- Bujutsu: A term for traditional martial arts.
- Bujutsu-ka: A martial arts practitioner.
- Budō: The martial ways. Used in reference to modern martial arts.

C
- Chikama: Close interval.
- Chūdan-no-kamae: The middle stance or on-guard position.
- Chūshin: The centre.

D
- Daihyōsha-sen: Representative match or sudden-death playoff.
- Dan: Rank.
- Debana-men: A technique in which the opponent's *men* is struck just as they are about to make an attack.
- Debana-waza: Techniques which are executed just as the opponent is about to attack.
- Dō: The plastron or body protector and target area.
- Dōjō: Training hall for the martial arts.

E
- En: Connection with the opponent.
- Enzan-no-metsuke: A term for one's gaze in kendo. Literally means "Looking at a far mountain", and implies looking at the opponent, but taking all of the surrounds in as well rather than focussing on one spot.

F
- Fumikomi: Stamp.
- Fumikomi-ashi: The lunging footwork used in kendo that finishes with a firm stamp on the floor.

G
- Gyaku-dō: Reverse *dō* strike.

H
- Hansei: Self-reflection.
- Harai: To ward off or slap the opponent's *shinai*.

GLOSSARY

- Harai-waza: Techniques in which the opponent's *shinai* is slapped out of the way first.
- Hasuji: The line of the strike and trajectory of the blade.
- Hikagami: The back of the knee.
- Hikitsuke: The act of snapping the rear foot up.
- Hiki-waza: Reverse techniques executed from close quarters.
- Hiraki-ashi: Type of foot work used for moving to the side.
- Hyaku-ren-ji-toku: An old adage that means "practise one hundred times in order memorise something".

I

- Ippon: A point.
- Ippon-shōbu: A match in which the first person to score one point is the winner.
- Issoku-ittō-no-maai: The spatial interval which literally means "one-step, one-sword".

J

- Ji-geiko: Free sparring or fencing practice.
- Jōgai-hansoku: Penalty for stepping out of bounds.

K

- Kakari-geiko: Attack practice.
- Kakarite: The attacker.
- Kamae: A stance or fighting posture.
- Kata-geiko: Kata (set forms) practice.
- Katate-zuki: One-handed thrust to the throat.
- Katsugi-men: Shouldering the *shinai* then striking *men*.
- Keiko: Traditional term for training in the martial arts and other arts.
- Ken: Sword.
- Kendō-ka: Kendo practitioner.
- Kensen: Tip of the sword of *shinai*.
- Kentai-itchi: Offence and defence are inseparably combined.
- Ki: Basic energy that exists in all living things.
- Kiai: Vocalisations and equilibrium of *ki*. Spirit.
- Kihon: Basics.
- Kihon-geiko: Training in fundamental techniques.
- Kihon-uchi: Basic striking.
- Ki-ken-tai-no-itchi: The unity of spirit, sword, and body.
- Kime: Decisiveness in a strike.
- Kirikaeshi: Basic practice method in kendo consisting of continuous strikes to the *men*.
- Kōbō-itchi: See *kentai-itchi*.
- Kote: The protective gauntlet. A target area in kendo.
- Kūkan-datotsu: Practice strikes into air.
- Kyū: The system of grades before *dan*.

M

- Maai: Spatial and time interval.
- Maki: To roll the *shinai*
- Men: The protective mask. A target area in kendo.
- Men-nuki-dō: A technique in which a *men* strike is avoided and countered with a strike to *dō*.
- Men-tore: The command to remove *men* at the end of training.
- Men-tsuke: The command to put on the *men*.

- Metsuke: Gaze, or use of the eyes.
- Mise-waza: Set-up techniques.
- Mokusō: Meditation.
- Morote-zuki: Two-handed thrust to the throat.
- Motodachi: The receiver in training.
- Mushin: The state of "no-mind".

N
- Nippon kendo kata: The set of ten prescribed forms.

O
- Ōji-waza: Counter-techniques.
- Okuri-ashi: Footwork that resembles a shuffle with the right foot forward.
- Osae: The suppress.
- Osae-waza: Techniques executed after suppressing the opponent's *shinai*.

R
- Rei: Bow or etiquette.
- Renzoku-waza: Continuous techniques.

S
- San-sappō: To kill the opponent's *shinai*, *waza*, and spirit.
- Sa-yū: Left and right.
- Seisei-dōdō: Fair and square.
- Seiza: Traditional method of sitting by kneeling.
- Seme: To apply pressure or assail the opponent.
- Seme-ai: The act of mutual probing to create openings in the opponent's defences.
- Senpai: A senior.
- Senpō: The first fighter in a team.
- Sensei: A teacher or instructor.
- Shiai: Match.
- Shiai-geiko: Match practice.
- Shiai-jō: The match court.
- Shikake-waza: Self-initiated techniques.
- Shinai: The bamboo practice sword used in kendo.
- Shinpan: Referees.
- Shinsa: Promotion examination.
- Shodachi: The first cut.
- Shodan: The first of the eight *dan* grades.
- Shugyō: Ascetic training.
- Suri-ashi: Sliding footwork.
- Sonkyo: The squatting position assumed before the commencement of a bout.
- Suriage-waza: A technique in which the opponent's attack is parried in a upward motion.
- Sute-waza: Throw-away techniques.

T
- Tabi: Split-toe socks or footwear.
- Tachisuji: The line or trajectory of the sword.
- Tai: Body.

GLOSSARY

- Taiatari: Body clash.
- Taikai: Tournament.
- Taisabaki: Body movement.
- Taishō: The final fighter in a team. The captain.
- Tare: Lower body protective equipment.
- Tenouchi: One's grip or way of holding the sword or *shinai*.
- Tobikomi-men: Striking *men* by leaping in.
- Tokui-waza: One's speciality technique.
- Tōma: Distant interval.
- Tsuba: Hand-guard at the base of the sword above the grip.
- Tsubazeriai: A tussle at close-quarters.
- Tsugi-ashi: A type of footwork.
- Tsuka: The grip or handle of a sword or *shinai*.
- Tsuki: A thrust to the throat.

U
- Uchikomi-geiko: Basic striking practice.
- Utte-hansei-utarete-kansha: A teaching in which the practitioner is encouraged to reflect when one strikes successfully, and be grateful when struck.

W
- Wakare: The command to separate.
- Waza: Technique.
- Waza-geiko: Technique practice.

Z
- Zanshin: Continued physical and mental alertness after striking.

INDEX

INDEX

ABOUT THE AUTHOR

Sotaro Honda

Born in 1972, Sotaro Honda graduated from Fukuoka University of Education in 1997 (M.Ed.) and the University of Gloucestershire in 2003 (Ph.D.). Kendo Renshi 7-dan. British Kendo National Team Coach (2002-2007). Competed in the All Japan Todofuken Taiko Kendo Tournament. Has taught kendo in Britain, China, Hong Kong, Italy, Russia, Singapore and Spain. Currently works at the Fukuoka University of Education as Associate Professor (Health and Physical Education). Head of the university kendo club. National Education University Kendo Federation Director.

Printed in the USA
CPSIA information can be obtained
at www.ICGtesting.com
LVHW080621171023
761194LV00020B/55

9 784907 009359